Akashic Field Affirmations – *Heal th*

Cover Designs & Graphics: Beth Turowski (www.bethturowski.com)

Editing By: Sheila K. Warwick, BS, MS Edu
Rogers State University, Claremore, OK

To request use permission for any materials in this book or additional information:

Martes Group, Inc.
705B SE Melody Lane #206
Lees Summit, MO 64063
816-841-4890

ISBN: 0-9772293-0-0

Akashic Field Affirmations

Heal the Past & Create your Future

By CJ Martes

"At the heart of each of us,
whatever our imperfections,
there exists a silent pulse of perfect rhythm,
a complex of wave forms and resonance,
which is absolutely individual and unique,
and yet which connects us
to everything in the universe."

~ George Leonard

TABLE OF CONTENTS

Introduction

Since I was a little girl I knew there was a purpose for being alive. I felt intensely connected to the divine creator as a child. I also knew I was here to do something important with my life to help others. This spiritual calling lay so deep inside me that I have been aware of it for as long as I can remember. I remember a distinct spiritual voice I believe was God speaking to me about many things and filling me with beautiful feelings on many levels.

I grew up in a very small town in Kansas. My family was Catholic and I went to Catholic school through my elementary school years. I attended church regularly with my family. The mysticism of the Catholic Church fascinated me as a child. During my school years, I often would sneak out of class to wander over to the cathedral to have conversations with God. This behavior was routine, much to the dismay of the nuns in charge of me that had to go looking for me from time to time.

When I was 7 or 8 I began to notice that I could see things in life that others did not. I had many visits with various relatives who had past away. They often gave me the mission to deliver final messages to my family. I could see energy around people and things. I often knew more than I should have rationally known about people I didn't know personally. My intuition about whether people were honest was usually never wrong.

Those that know me well understand that I have always been passionate about my role in life and my purpose for being. I have lost my path and way numerous times but always returned to serving myself and others. There were even times I believe that God grabbed me by the back of my neck and firmly planted me back on my path whenever I'd wander too far. What a grace that has been even though I may have resented it at the time.

During many trials in my life, I have always tried to see the bigger picture and expand my own point of view. Even with the ability to see the grander view, I have still felt my limits, pushed myself to a crazy extreme, cried many tears and struggled with the most common of human questions: *Why am I here? What is the true meaning of this situation? Why do bad things always seem to happen to me? Why can't I just go home? Will I ever be truly happy?*

I'm not sure I can answer all the above questions even now. Eventually I had to learn to be as true to myself as possible. There's a cliché that we've all heard many, many times...*You can't love anyone else until you truly love yourself.* I eventually took this advice to heart and began to heal myself through being more self-loving and allowing myself to heal.

In recent years we've all seen a wonderful expansion of spiritual consciousness taking root in the world. It's been truly amazing to see how much we've evolved over the past 10 years. We now live in a new age where we are actively trying to clear our fears, striving to grow and are ultimately trying to heal ourselves and this planet.

During this past decade we have sought to expand our own consciousness, awareness and understanding of our lives and find our truest selves. I see this movement as a beautiful opportunity. It makes me very hopeful for our future and the future of all our children.

This unique time of growth gives us all the opportunity to engage in activities and practices that can expand our personal awareness of ourselves and our world. Especially with the Internet as a tool, we can all learn about new healing methods, profound philosophical view points and even the latest quantum scientific discoveries much faster than before.

All of this growth and new information makes me happy to be alive at such a pivotal time in the world as we know it.

As I have looked at my own journey and those of the people I am blessed to know, I realized at last what my life's work would be. This important self-discovery happened only in the last several years.

Regardless of how elusive my true path was, I desired with all my heart to do spiritual and intuitively based work for others that was practical for a person's everyday life. I wanted my work to be meaningful and present the greatest opportunity for tremendous growth in people's lives. I really wanted to make an impact by offering services that really help people on their often complicated journeys through human experience.

This desire led me eventually to the source of all our soul memories: to the origination of our subconscious defenses, the potential for our future, and the vast sea of quantum information called the *Akashic Field*.

I have been working for a couple years with people all over the world using the method I developed called Akashic Field Therapy SM. I help people to identify and release patterns that block them from fully expressing their authentic self.

This work has been a deeper blessing for me. I found that all my clients' situations in life that they were trying to overcome, taught me tremendously about my own life. I recognize now that every person I meet is a mirror for what I most need to know.

In my work with the Akashic Field, I choose to be a mirror of information for those I work with in order to help them break free from whatever is holding them back.

I decided to write this book about the basics of working with the Akashic Field in your everyday life. Many people have been asking me over the past year: What can I do to access the Akashic Field myself?

I have written this book to address the need for people to take advantage of this way of healing the past and creating a better future.

I have written this book to be used by anyone. It doesn't matter your spiritual background or knowledge level. You can use this book effectively to shift a lot of negative energy out of your life and imprint positive energies into your Akashic Field.

You can use the information and tools in this book to heal your past. If you were drawn to this book, then it is not an accident. Everything happens for a reason. You were meant to become aware of this energy available to you and harness it to make your life a better place.

I appreciate your purchase of this book and wish you many future blessings. I know in my heart and soul that you can make your life a better place and create a healthy, positive future for yourself and others.

I truly wish happiness and abundance for you on your glorious journey through life!

International Healer and Author
Developer of Akashic Field Therapy [SM]

Chapter One

A Journey toward the Book of Life

"Our Creator would never have made such lovely days,
and given us the deep hearts to enjoy them,
above and beyond all thought,
unless we were meant to be immortal"

- Nathaniel Hawthorne

We all have a story to tell. Every person on the earth has many, many stories nestled inside the experiences of their lives. Some people's stories are happy; others are sad, inspiring, tragic or empowering. Whatever the story is we all have them, and we are creating more each and every day.

If you compare your stories to someone else's, you may find them similar. Our stories connect us to everyone else in deep and meaningful ways. Those who have passed on from life as we understand it, leave their stories behind as a memento of who they were and what they accomplished.

If you look at your own story, what does it say about you? Even when you are no longer here, your stories live on forever in the hearts of those who knew you. Many believe that we are immortal in spirit and that we are never destroyed even when our human bodies have long past from the earth. I knew in my heart as a child that we are infinite in our true form and that we are far more than the physical vehicle we use to travel through life.

There are many beliefs in the world about what actually happens at the moment we are finished on our life journey. Perhaps we will never truly know until we experience those moments for ourselves.

Through major accomplishments in modern medical science we make great strides to enhance the longevity of our physical bodies, cure diseases and hopefully make our lives a bit easier. All of these things do not guarantee our immortality however.

Why do we strive for immortality or cling to human existence in so many ways? That's a personal question that many of us could spend a lifetime trying to answer. It's also a question with no wrong answer either which I love the most.

During my own quest to answer many important philosophical questions, I stumbled across our part of immortality and didn't know it at the time. In all I've learned, I have become convinced that we do have a measure of immortality not only because of our divine souls granted by our creator, but also within every single human experience we have while living.

You are always remembered not only in the minds of your friends and family members; accomplishments that are notable, but in the memory of the universe itself. In essence we leave an imprint with our human existence that endures forever. This life imprint is called your "Book of Life". The terms Akashic Records, Akashic Field or Akashic Chronicles are all a representation of your life imprint as well.

Ten years ago was the first time I recall reading an article about the subject of the Akashic Records. As with most things having to do spirituality, I was fascinated by these ancient stories of our histories being recorded. At first, I didn't even know what the word "Akashic" meant.

Akasha is a Sanskrit word meaning "sky", "space" or "aether". The Akashic Records are, therefore, said to be a collection of wisdom that is stored in the "aether". What "aether" really means is a type of energy or an area of space outside our ability to perceive it with our human senses.

The Akashic Records are said to have existed since the beginning of the planet. Just as we have various types of libraries in the world, there are said to exist various Akashic Records associated with humans, animals, plants etc. Most historical writings refer to the Akashic Records in the area of our human experience. Mystics and sages have long maintained that an interconnecting, cosmic energy field exists at the roots of reality that conserves and conveys information, a field known as the Akashic Records.

Many ancient cultures also believed in the existence of the Akashic Records. This belief was held by many ancient peoples around the world including the Tibetans, Egyptians, Greeks, Chinese, Hebrews, Christians and Mayans. Even priests of the Himalayas prior to Buddhism knew that each soul recorded every moment of its existence in a "book", and that if one attuned oneself properly then one could read or view them. In ancient Egypt, those who could read the Akasha were advisors to the Pharaohs on daily activities.

I recall thinking to myself how amazing it was that all of our life experiences were recorded somewhere "out there". When I was thinking about it, I envisioned the Akashic Records as a huge library with an infinite number of books about all the events in every person's lifetime. During my research I discovered that there were people in our modern era who offered intuitive readings that accessed a person's "book of life".

I have never had anyone perform such a reading for me, but I know many who have. I didn't pursue it for myself because my entire understanding of them was that someone would tell me stories about my past lives. Since I already remembered a great deal about my own past lies, I didn't really need someone to give me that information. I started having dreams and recollection of my past lives as early as 8 years old. I remember my first past life memory as one in ancient Egypt which led me to actively study the history and culture.

It wasn't until several years ago this subject of the Akashic Records would resurface again. Several synchronous events led me back to this subject area. It was an amazing flow of energy that brought everything together for me. Those events would place me on the spiritual path and what would eventually become my life's work.

In order to explain fully how I ended up writing this book, I feel like you should know a few things beforehand about my own spiritual history.

I had a very amazing and challenging childhood. I was born with very strong spiritual gifts that I didn't always understand. I was very intuitive, had dreams that would come true, had many conversations with deceased relatives and could hear angels speaking to me a lot of the time. My parents, aunts and uncles and teachers often had a difficult time understanding what I would communicate to them freely about whatever I was seeing or hearing. I didn't understand until the age of 35 that there were other children like me called *Indigo Children*.

Finding out that I was an Indigo Child really changed my life. It really helped me to know that there were some real explanations for the gifts I had and my intense motivation to find my "path". It was also immensely helpful to know I was not as alone as I have felt at times. I recall using my gifts very naturally my whole childhood. My gifts presented some challenges as I got older. I often said things to others without realizing it was out of the ordinary. I often knew things about people that they said I shouldn't be able to know without them telling me. This sometimes caused fears in those around me. Of course other times kids thought it was "cool".

At some point in our lives, we all lose a bit of our childhood innocence. It was hard growing up being viewed as different from other children. It was also hard for me to understand people who were not as loving as me or the cruelty that sometimes people can have towards themselves or others.

Most of this started around the age of 13. I was getting older and trying to figure out who I was just like any typical teenager. Through this process of growing up, I had a very hard time having my spiritual gifts. It was like getting too much input all the time, and I remember feeling more and more "crazy" as time went on. At the time, I had no one to discuss such things with so I'm sure that made it even more difficult for me to understand. At times I longed to have no spiritual gifts, so I could be like other people.

Around the age of 15 my parents went through a messy divorce and my entire world was turned upside down. I was a very angry, young woman and resented most things about my life.

I even wondered why God would put me here in such a place. Was I being punished? I felt abandoned and separate from the single most beautiful thing in my world. I longed to return home to become one with that beautiful energy and discard this confusing human world filled with pain and suffering.

This emotional trauma and my feelings of separation eventually led me to feel like shoving my gifts as far away from me as possible. In my teenage mind, they were the problem and not the cure for my issues. Since I had a choice in the matter, I purposely left my spiritual gifts in the closet and didn't allow them to emerge until many years later.

I had a rocky life after my parents divorce. I was still trying to find myself in a strange and often disappointing world. I went through many relationships and several abusive marriages until finding my life partner David whom I am still with today.

He and I met when I was 25 years old. He said it was "love at first sight". I loved that he made me laugh. We both had hard lives full of disappointment before we met. Finding each other granted us some stability to both our lives. I actually felt for the first time that someone loved me just the way I am. This made a huge difference for me and helped to heal much of my own feelings of separation.

I began to believe finally that my life might actually become happier. It was the first time since being a teenager I had felt that way. In the midst of this freeing feeling however, I went through a sudden shift in my own awareness that I never expected.

Things were finally going well in my life but as we built our life together and we made plans for our future, I became more and more upset inside. It's difficult to describe, but it was like I began to see all my past traumatic and painful situations like pictures in a photo album. I could not seem to escape these images in my mind though I tried very hard.

I remember thinking that it made no sense to feel this way at all. Things were finally becoming good in my life yet here I was feeling awful instead of happy.

I've learned that it's normal when we don't understand something to fight against it. In retrospect, I know now I was judging myself for my pain. I was feeling weak for it, rather than understanding that with all I had been through, I had a right feel this way.

I fought a great battle inside my own mind about my conflicted emotions, but it only made matters worse and I fell into depression. Over several months, my depression grew much worse. I eventually could not find the energy to get out of my bed very often.

My dear husband tried to cheer me up with teddy bears, flowers, cards and sweet kisses. I'm sure he felt as helpless as I did. I knew he loved me but it didn't matter. I wanted the answers to free myself but couldn't find them. Everything seemed gray and hopeless.

I eventually tried traditional therapy, depression medication and holistic remedies. Each day all my past traumatic memories circled in my mind like a group of vultures looking for their next meal. I felt something had to shift soon because the cycle was essentially driving me crazy. Luckily something did, but it came in a way I would have not have anticipated.

I spent a lot of time alone during this period of time since being near other people made me uncomfortable. Then one day my life changed. I was sitting by myself in our upstairs master bedroom. To the left of our queen size bed were two big recliners that sat in front of a television set with a small table between them.

David and I would often spend our evenings watching television after the kids had gone to bed. I sat in my usual chair on the right side rocking myself back and forth. I was sitting there thinking about how much my life really sucked right now. I was so upset that I couldn't simply snap out of it. I was so frustrated that I honestly thought of nothing else.

As I sat there with my spiraling thoughts for about a half hour, I eventually came back to the same place I had started: "Nothing I was experiencing made sense. I was so sad in my heart. I was so hurt and nothing could fix it".

I felt exhausted as I slumped into my padded chair. I then said aloud as I put my arms out, "I am so tired of hurting! I just can't do this anymore!"

My arms fell into my lap. I then covered my face and started sobbing. I eventually stopped crying after awhile. I sat there simply numb and tired.

Then, without warning, I heard a quiet but clear voice come from out of nowhere. It was almost like hearing my own voice but the sound was somewhat different. The voice said, "You are not hurting. You are healing."

I was startled to hear this phrase so clearly in my room. I quickly looked around to see if someone was there. Of course no one was there, but it felt like there should have been.

I thought about those spoken words carefully. What was said had never occurred to me during those several months of intense pain. After a few moments of consideration, I said aloud, "Well if I'm healing instead of hurting, then I can't do it alone."

I raised my hands up toward the ceiling and said, "Someone please help me". Of course I didn't expect the phantom voice to answer me. I had learned through my whole life not to count on anyone else but me. I had survived terrible and often dangerous situations all on my own.

The amazing thing was I received a response, and the one I received was quite unexpected. I felt an immediate rush of peace and love flow through my entire body. My fingertips were tingling with energy. For the first time since my childhood, I felt my connection to God again. I felt God's presence all around me. My loneliness left me. I was home again.

What happened after this is almost another story itself. To make it short, every bit of my spiritual gifts which I had locked away flew out of that closet and returned to me all at once. I will always consider this experience the day of my great "awakening"; the beginning of my wonderful journey toward wholeness.

My story is perhaps a dramatic one. I have other life stories that are not this profound. I share the story of my "awakening" because it reveals the difference changing a single word can make. It changed my entire life. I am still fascinated that such a minor shift in perception allowed my healing to finally take place.

I never could have seen this were it not for my spiritual "education" that day. My chosen word at that time was *hurting*. I saw only my pain. I didn't like it and wanted it to simply go away. I was afraid it would go on and on with no end. I was afraid the intense feelings would consume me so I tried to run away from them.

The new word *healing* had a beginning and an end unlike my chosen word *hurting*. It's still so amazing to me that in a single moment, I went from feeling like a trapped animal in pain to being fully liberated to heal myself. The healing didn't happen overnight, but my willingness and openness to new growth opportunities did.

That profound moment became the essential beginning of those synchronous events I mentioned earlier that led me to study the subject of the Akashic Records. After my "awakening, I started to work with people using my spiritual gifts to help them have a better life.

My new insights allowed me see something about life I had not been able to see before. After this, I endeavored to learn as much as I could about the release of past traumas, emotional healing, and different perceptions of reality.

Everything in my life was broken down in my mind in terms of varied perceptions of reality. I sought to see the truth of my life. I did not want to keep my old perceptions that were based on past traumas and fears.

Using my own experiences, I hoped to help people shift their negative perceptions in the spiritual work I was doing. I was fascinated to see the many differences in the perceptions of each person I met. At that time, I saw the entire realm of all human experience as two sets of perceptions: those that were positive and those that were negative. I tried very earnestly over the next several years to heal my own past traumas and create a more positive perception in my life.

Life felt good to me most of the time. While using my spiritual gifts to help others, I also continued to work through my issues as best I could and honored my healing more each time I encountered an opportunity.

Eventually I would be guided towards the next step of my journey. About 6 months after "awakening", I met a chiropractor who would soon become one of the most influential teachers of my life. He was offering a training program in vibrational healing.

I made the decision to enroll in his Vibrational Healing Training Program which altogether was 18 months of intensive learning about subtle energy, human energy systems, working with directed energy techniques, anatomy and much more. I attended the training program in 1997. In addition to all the knowledge I gained from the program, I also learned to use dowsing to access information which would be a very important tool later on. I appreciated Larry's guidance and teaching so much.

After completing the program, I added vibrational healing to my client practice. I worked with many clients to identify physical imbalances and blocks in various subtle energies. I used specific directed energy techniques to help clear them. This medical/intuitive work became the foundation for my future work.

After working in this area, I felt I needed to move towards the realm of habitual patterns, psychology, and emotional release. Most of my client session work using vibrational healing dealt with subtle energy, how we store trauma in our physical body and how we pick up discordant energies from our environment or other people.

I also used my intuitive insights to guide this process with my clients. Over time the gifts from my childhood were back and much stronger than before. I soon found myself wanting to go deeper with my work and balance it between the physical, mental and spiritual. Everyone who knows me understands that I'm a very spiritually driven person at times. Since feeling called by God to make the world a better place, I've obeyed that voice even when I haven't had the slightest idea how to accomplish it.

In 1999 I read a book written by an associate of mine named Anne Brewer. It was entitled: *Breaking Free to Health, Wealth & Happiness*. This led me to learn about her healing method called Soul Clearing. Her method uses a series of charts that access emotional blocks in the Akashic Records that appear in life as limiting patterns of behavior.

Performing this work seemed to be a logical next step in my client practice. I decided to take Anne's basic and advanced trainings to learn to use this method as a tool for my client work.

I was profoundly fascinated about the Akashic Records after doing Soul Clearings. I am by nature a very curious person so I continued my research. Since childhood I always needed to know why things worked a certain way or how they functioned. I wanted to learn more in order to continue working in the area of emotional trauma and behavioral patterning. I knew in my heart I wanted to delve deeper into working with emotional trauma but was unsure how to go about it.

The final piece of the puzzle fell into place at a Christmas party hosted by some friends of mine. My husband David and I attended and were really enjoying the party. Some point that evening I looked over at my friend hosting the party who was with another friend. They were both hunched over a laptop computer at the kitchen table. We had just finished dinner.

I was curious about what they were discussing, so I walked over to them. I don't even remember what they were talking about, only what caught my eye next. My host was intently looking for a computer file to show her. As he scrolled through his files, my eyes focused on a particular file name. I immediately pointed to his screen saying, "Ooh what is that?" The file title was: *Science and the Akashic Field.*

Looking back, it probably seemed abrupt when I cut into the conversation and pointed at the file asking what it was. My friend told me it was a book recently released by a well-known physicist named *Ervin Laszlo*. It was about his theory of the Akashic Field or what he termed the "A-Field". Something clicked inside me and I knew it was important.

I wrote down the name of the book so I wouldn't forget. I was so excited and wanted to get a copy as soon as possible. I knew inside it had to do with my life path and purpose. I asked for it the next day as a possible Christmas gift. To my delight, I received it from my husband on December 25.

I was not surprised that David picked the book up for me at such short notice since he's always very supportive of my spiritual work and the many subjects I've studied over the years.

I quickly read the entire book the next day. I was very inspired and knew what I needed to do. It led me to start blending my own spiritual experiences, education and client healing background with the realm of quantum physics and the Akashic Records.

Laszlo's book contains a theory that the Akashic Records were not just a story but real and equivalent to a zero-point energy field that is imprinted with all human experiences. I was astounded to see this information coming from a well-known, Nobel Peace Prize winning scientist.

As I studied his information, I imagined that the existence of the Akashic Records would be in serious doubt by the scientific community since there was no way to prove its existence through experiments and testing.

My research into Laszlo's work led me to believe that the Akashic Records are impressed or encoded into a quantum energy field. This information is continually rewritten based on our choices, thoughts, emotions, and fears.

I have read in various books that early scientific pioneers have long searched for what they called the "aether", or that "substance" that exists within the vacuum of space. These scientists' "aether" also spelled "ether" is also translated of course to mean "Akasha". Were they in essence searching for the Akashic Records?

Eventually, in more modern times, scientists discovered that the elusive "aether" was a new realm of time and space called the quantum vacuum. They discovered also that this vacuum is a super dense, frictionless medium that carries light and all the universal forces of nature through it as energy. The quantum vacuum exists at a subatomic level, well beyond our ability to measure it. Laszlo later added to this discovery by his theory that it was not only filled with energy but imprinted with vast amounts of information.

The most notable mystic and psychic who routinely assessed the Akashic Records in the form of readings for individuals was *Edgar Cayce*. Edgar Cayce lived from 1877 to 1945 and during his lifetime performed thousands of such readings for people all over the world. I had first heard of his work through my vibrational healing training from my teacher.

Cayce was very well respected for all of his intuitive insights. He greatly influenced the lives of his clients. He also influenced the holistic health field with some of the natural remedies he accessed from the Akashic Records. It is easy to study his work because he carefully documented each person's reading and follow-up for many years past a client's initial session with him.

A full database of these client cases is searchable online through a paid membership in his foundation (*www.edgarcayce.org*). Because of his work, he gained perhaps the most concrete evidence and information about the way the Akashic Records work for each of us.

Cayce believed that the Akashic Records contained a history of every soul since the dawn of creation. These records connect us to each other he often said. They contain the stimulus for every symbol, archetype or mythic story that has ever heavily touched the patterns of human behavior.

When asked where the records reside, Cayce would say they exist within "the skein of space and time" and told many people interested in his work that the "records are everywhere". He further believed that the records are inscribed on some kind of "etheric energy" similar in nature to the energy of thought.

Cayce believed that revealing the past through his readings was useful to bring about conscious awareness of the soul's growth. He never stopped emphasizing that the records are written by each of us by our own free will and the choices we make in the present moment.

Cayce explained that the Akashic Records not only store everything in the past of an individual but they also contain all the future possibilities and potentials for our lives. He believed that we basically call into potential an array of possible futures as we interact with daily life and learn subconsciously from the data that has already been accumulated.

His view that all future potentials for us already exist in the Akashic Records is strikingly similar to a view that would emerge many decades later in Laszlo's A-Field theory. This also further supports the idea that our thoughts do indeed create our reality and that it is our perceptions that drive what is "real" for each of us.

Similar to the views that Cayce had about the Akashic Records, Laszlo theorizes that the quantum vacuum may not only be a super dense sea of frictionless energy but also a sea of information conveying the "historical experience of matter."

His theory concludes that the Akashic Field is real and is equivalent to a zero-point energy field that underlies space itself. Laszlo states that the quantum vacuum essentially, "generates the holographic field that is the memory of the universe." He also believes that the A-Field is proof of the interconnected nature of our world.

Another similarity which is interesting to mention is that Cayce also believed that the Akashic Records "connected us to each other" and that the universe was indeed "orderly" or informed.

Laszlo further suggests that the A-Field is like a hologram that is imprinted with all that has been or ever will be similar to Cayce's assertion that the Akashic Records contained all that was and all the potentials for our future.

As I put all the pieces together, I realized that my own method and practice was being born. I was thrilled to finally find my calling and be able to share this information with others. Akashic Field Therapy℠ was developed later that same year.

It may be hard to imagine what this vast energy field really looks like. As Cayce said, "the records are everywhere". We are never disconnected from it. I imagine this to be like an invisible super computer network with myriads of data filled pathways or a vast grid. Each pathway leads to other pathways and so on.

Another way to imagine it would be to think of a 4D holographic grid that literally contains every single thought, event and action that has been experienced. It also contains all of the potential experiences we could have in the future. Depending on the choices we make the field's grid activates and assists to create whatever reality is available to us.

This stored information is subconsciously accessed through an intricate array of interconnecting patterns like a spider web. Your individual expressions of self are imprinted onto this energy along with every other individual's. Though your experiences are not mixed with someone else's they are connected within the same field of energy. Those who are considered psychic or intuitive can tap into this field at will to help provide information to people.

The Akashic Field in itself gives us a fair measure of immortality if you think about it. All that you've ever been, are now, and ever may be is there waiting to be accessed. You are a part of the enduring memory of the universe. With or without a physical being, you exist forever. For those that believe we live many lifetimes, it's easier to understand how this could be possible with the Akashic Field.

The Akashic Field affects our daily lives substantially. If you have a lot of positive energy in the field, then you may find it easier to create whatever you desire. Likewise, if there is a lot of unresolved trauma or fear, the grid becomes blocked and can limit you from accessing a wider array of possibilities. Having energy blocked in the Akashic Field can shift or narrow your perception of reality.

The profound experience I had with my own perception shift of the word *hurting* to *healing* is a perfect example of this. I was unable to see the other potential, *healing,* because my unresolved trauma and fears had blocked that viewpoint from being available to me. There are many similar examples to be found in everyone's life.

With Laszlo's recent scientific theory of the Akashic Field, all the ancient knowledge written about the Akashic Records or "The Book of Life" are shifted from mere myths to an integral part of our world.

This became the foundation for my life's work. I wanted to be able to identify and locate the stored traumas in order to release and rewrite the energy stored in a person's Akashic Field. I knew that if this energy field is written with our thoughts and actions, then it is reasonable to believe that it can be accessed more consciously and thus rewritten.

My new realization became a catalyst for me. I endeavored to gain a greater understanding of the Akashic Field and its inherent properties. I was inspired with the belief that somehow we could directly access this important history of ourselves in order to facilitate an energetic shift from negative energies to positive potentials in our lives.

I knew inside that if we could make the conscious choice to do this, then the negative behaviors and past traumas we are still storing in our Akashic Field could be liberated and healed. By gaining this information and using it, my intent was to help more and more people to release unresolved trauma and increase the spiritual energy available for creating positive life outcomes.

Within a short period of time I developed Akashic Field Therapy SM. This method allows me to gain direct access to this vast sea of information by utilizing 17 charts that interpret possible emotional and traumatic states, negative beliefs, self-condemning thoughts, subconscious blocks and other associated patterns of behavior.

Dowsing a set of grid-like charts was the best way to identify and then interpret the energies of the Akashic Field. Energy had to be translated from the Akashic Field into possible human words and experiences. It was especially challenging to make the charts as inclusive as possible of all negative thoughts, emotional states and traumas that could be there.

The method and chart system were created drawing upon various theories and methodologies: Behavioral Psychology (*looking for specific human behaviors that inhibit personal growth*); Integral Psychology (*addressing the 4 quadrants of human evolution*); Quantum Theory (*our perception of reality is based on our previous experiences*); Spirituality (*accessing our powerful, divine, and all-knowing nature*); Soul Clearing (*as developed by Anne Brewer for freeing patterns and using charts to access the Akashic Records*); and Vibrational Medicine (*human energy systems, transformational tools, directed energy techniques and the power of prayer or intention*).

My results in various client sessions suggest that any work directly with the Akashic Field can provide a concrete foundation for positive personal transformation and change.

Through interpretation of the information that is located for an individual, I have the ability to interpret this energetically stored information and convey it in simple, relevant, and understandable terms. This gives conscious awareness to life affecting patterns that were previously held in the subconscious so they can be worked with directly.

Another key to the great insight that can be gained from the Akashic Field is discovering what a person's soul was attempting to learn through the sometimes traumatic events in their past.

How many times have we all thought, I could get over this bad situation if only I knew why it happened? What could I have been trying to learn? As human beings we all need to understand the past events in our lives. We need a deeper meaning to relate to. Working with the Akashic Field can help find the meaning we are looking for.

Some patterns can be liberated energetically with proper intention. Other patterns have to be worked with for a more extended period of time. The most effective tool so far has been the use of affirmations to help imprint positive attributes in place of the negative patterns previously found.

Using such affirmations quickly became one of the most important tools for allowing my clients to be in control of their own healing processes and take responsibility for it. During hundreds of client sessions, I began writing customized affirmations as homework for a person to shift deeply ingrained patterns of behavior that were identified. These worked very well to help shift the negative patterns to positive potentials.

The effectiveness of affirmations and the request of people to have resources to work directly with the Akashic Field themselves led to the creation of the book you hold in your hands now.

Through my recent work I believe that we are on the verge of a new revolution of human consciousness. Our newest understanding about the Akashic Field unites each of our individual perceptions of reality into a unified whole. It grants us the ability to uncover the information we need to resolve any issues that are still unresolved. With the right information, you can resolve stored trauma from your past in order to unlock positive potentials for your future.

The Akashic Field and your own story play an important role in the growth experiences you have. What does your story tell? What are you trying to learn? What can you create in your future? How can you improve the quality of your life?

All the answers you seek are just waiting there to be discovered.

Chapter Two

The Doorway to the Akashic Field

There are only two ways to live . . .
one is as though nothing is a miracle. . .
the other is as if everything is.

- Albert Einstein

Every moment of the day we have choices to make. As our lives become more and more complicated that statement escalates into a crescendo of life moments just passing us by. We become so busy that something kicks in automatically in order to get everything done. It's like being set on an internal auto-pilot.

Being distracted is so easy for any of us to do. It does seem that life is becoming more and more complicated these days. We make plans for time to spend in meditation or prayer but something comes up and we set it aside. We hear so often from various spiritual teachers about being in the present moment. This is very, very challenging to do on a consistent basis. I try but can't always stay there myself. I have four children at home and this issue can be my greatest challenge at times. They give me a lot of practice being fully present in the moment to help them with all their needs.

It's easy to become more and more subject to our automated responses in our daily life when there's so much to get done. When life becomes this way, the subconscious mind is steering the ship rather than our conscious mind. So much is driven by the subconscious that even with our conscious will we cannot always meet our goals in life. This has always perplexed me.

The purpose of my work has been to provide the answers to why we can try to move forward but find ourselves unable to do so. Many of my answers came in my work with the Akashic Field.

There are three types of consciousness within each of us: subconscious, conscious and super-conscious. The subconscious mind is most characterized by your automatic responses. The conscious mind is best described as your independent will. The super-conscious is the "all knowing" divine nature in each of us. Many people call this your high-self.

Of these three consciousness aspects, it is your <u>subconscious</u> that accesses your soul memories directly from the Akashic Field. This "soul database" is like an imprinted hologram of energy with everything about you stored there.

In order to fully explain the process it is helpful that you understand the nature of the subconscious mind. It defends you against harm, is not logical or reasonable. Like a child who takes everything literally, it regulates all involuntary responses, accesses your soul memories, and does not necessarily change with your conscious mind's independent will. It is also responsible for your inherent creativity.

The subconscious realm of your consciousness is that which separates you from your immediate consciousness. It <u>is not</u> subject to recall at will. It <u>is</u> characterized by latent, or unconscious memories, or stimuli too weak to enter into your conscious awareness.

Try to think about your life on a daily basis. There are thousands of thoughts, ideas and actions that are driven by your subconscious mind. Most of your thoughts in a given day are not really conscious ones. It is estimated that on average a person has as many as 60,000 separate thoughts per day.

Whether you realize it or not much of who you are in the world is influenced by your subconscious mind. For the average person it is estimated that up to 90% of their awareness about life operates at a subconscious level all day long, every day.

Think also about all the experiences that you've had in your life. These experiences are stored as soul memories within the Akashic Field. All experiences blend together to create a unique set of perceptions, beliefs, fears and opinions. This blending becomes your unique set of filters. Your choices in life are influenced by these filters. It can be easy to see why most people live in the past on continual basis without even realizing it.

I don't want to give the subconscious mind a bad reputation since it serves us very well and performs important functions for us. The subconscious mind ensures that we don't have to think about making our heart beat or inhaling to taking a breath.

The subconscious mind also serves as our protector, trying to keep us from harm. Here's an example of the usefulness of our subconscious:

> *A man was walking on the African savannah one day traveling from his particular village to the next. After awhile, he spotted a large tiger just ahead of him. Just as he stopped, the tiger spotted him and came running toward him. He ran away immediately to get to safety.*
>
> *The moment the tiger was seen by the man, his subconscious mind leapt to action for the body, mobilizing various hormones such as adrenaline to get him moving more quickly. If it didn't do this, the man would have been eaten by the tiger because he would still be standing there trying to consciously think about what to do next.*

In addition to the many body related functions that are regulated by your subconscious, other things such as your emotional defenses are controlled too. Whenever something happens to you externally, your subconscious instantly accesses your soul memories from The Akashic Field. It matches up your current experiences with past ones. If there is trauma associated with the match, it will try to protect you from harm by triggering defense mechanisms. This association occurs all day every day.

The Akashic Field holds your individual hologram - your database of information. Your subconscious mind accesses this hologram making no discernment between when the information was stored in the past and the present moment you are experiencing right now. So the traumatic experience is just as real to you as if it were currently happening.

There is a limited amount of our memories actually stored in our physical brain. It helps to process our soul memories as they are accessed by the subconscious. Our thoughts and resulting choices are generated in the brain. These choices are governed by our conscious mind. For most people, the subconscious drives the flow of their lives. Very little work is done with the conscious mind unless we know ourselves well enough. In order to do this, we must take time to look at our defensive reactions and our emotions.

The way the information stored in the Akashic Field is accessed works something like this:

> *An external event happens to you; your brain begins processing the information; the subconscious mind accesses soul memory from the Akashic Field attempting to find a common match with the situation; whether a positive or negative, an emotion rises out of our subconscious in response. Depending on how suppressed our emotions are dictates whether or not the feelings enter our conscious awareness at all. If you have a defensive reaction, then your subconscious is trying to protect you from something perceived as harmful.*

It's important to understand that your Akashic life hologram contains a balance of negative and positive energies or blocking versus growth opportunities. This field of energy is in constant fluctuation based on your life actions, thoughts and choices. It is like a mathematical equation that is striving to reach a harmonious positive balance.

You can look for blocking energy by recognizing the repeating patterns in your life. Have you ever wondered why the same thing is happening over and over again? The necessary completion of unresolved issues in the Akashic Field is the answer.

If you do not fully resolve (balance) that which is unresolved (unbalanced), they will be triggered again and again until you do. This is an inherent energetic process in your human experience.

Every event in our lives has a purpose or soul level intention associated with it. These growth opportunities are meant to teach us more about ourselves. Sometimes we do not complete the entire process of learning. This leaves negative, unresolved patterns of energies sitting in our Akashic Field. Over time this negative information accumulates and can ultimately cover up whatever we were trying to learn.

When we look externally out into the world, we are constantly judging things as good or bad. It is our judgments based on the dualistic nature of our lives that govern what is recorded into the Akashic Field. This is the basic dualism in our lives when we continue to place things into separate baskets in our awareness. The division we make is just an illusion we create. There is no real dualism in life. All things merge into one single energy of creation.

For instance, I got the raise today, so that's good. Somebody cut me off in traffic, that's bad. We have this constant decision-making that we're doing about whether things are positive or negative. As those things come into our experience, and we have either positive or negative thoughts we are dictating what is stored into the Akashic Field as growth or what patterns will be stored that may limit us.

We have so much data that is being processed that we don't even realize most of it in a conscious manner. We have our past memories, perception filters, defensive reactions, fears, emotions and thoughts. The true source of all our information can be found within in the Akashic Field.

Unresolved issues are focused on by the subconscious more readily than future potentials since they are the basis of our fears. This energy system is designed to allow you the opportunity to resolve negative patterns which have not been liberated and transformed into growth. When these issues are resolved the quantum energy is shifted from the negative to create access to even more positive future potentials.

When many unresolved negative experiences exist in the Akashic Field, they block our ability to pull positive potentials into our life experience. This narrows our more conscious perception of all our available choices.

This is why we can be consciously moving forward with our goals and dreams but find ourselves blocked from manifesting or creating the future we desire.

Every life experience, everything that has ever happened to you, even the filtered out information, is all stored there. So as you go through daily life, everything that you see, everything that you're taking in, every experience that you have, is writing and rewriting into the Akashic Field constantly.

You are accessing and storing information faster than the fastest process you can even imagine. Every time you're getting a new awareness about yourself, you're actually freeing energy out and putting new energy in. It's exactly like a computer. We put in to the field; we take out. Over time, if we don't resolve our issues or get to what I call the *soul growth opportunity* then the patterns remain until we do.

We often gain this type of higher awareness of life situations by discovering for ourselves the answers to common questions like: Why did that happen? Why did I choose to experience this? If we are moving too fast in our life, then we can store tremendous amounts of trauma. We can store more negative emotions rather than positive ones. If this is done then your soul memories can continue to pile up and thus block greater positive energy in your life.

Why do we store so much negative information? During each soul growth experience in life that occurs, we often leave matters unbalanced or unresolved. This is because we may judge those experiences as bad or undesirable especially if we are unable to see the greater good that will come from it. If this negative view is not resolved, it can cause negative patterns to be stored in association with those growth experiences. It is this discernment process or judgment of our experiences that can lead to stored negative patterns in the Akashic Field.

Over time these negative patterns can build up and thus reinforce contraction or fear rather than expansion of a person's consciousness through love and understanding. The truth is we are simply carrying around patterns that inhibit us from continuing our growth processes. This can limit our available options or prevent us from making changes in our life, even when we are consciously trying to do so.

Our souls' intention for growth can become covered up by our unresolved trauma or negative judgments of the original life situation. Often, a lot of traumatic or negative energies become associated with whatever you're trying to learn. This association can block you from accessing positive future potentials in your life. Perhaps you cannot get anywhere in your career or find that you have a hard time creating good relationships in your life, it can mean that there are these various negative energies or experiences that are still residing in the Akashic Field waiting for some resolution.

The good part of the entire process is that life is going to present an opportunity for you to resolve that energy or balance that equation later on. So if you leave something unresolved, life will provide you another opportunity at some point later on. So when we have repeating patterns, things that happen to us over and over again, it's that beautiful divine process of life finding a way to allow us to resolve those issues, to come to higher consciousness about them.

In daily life the Akashic Field is an integral part of our processes. We are all responding energetically to what each other needs. We are able to do so because of energetically encoded messages in the Akashic Field. Whether it is something that is traumatic or something that is happy, life's response at the soul level is to give you just what you need every time.

When things appear to be falling apart, it's hard to think to ourselves, "this is all perfect for me," but it's true. This concept took me awhile to fully believe in, but now I do. I had to let go of the attachment I had to figuring out the lessons while I was still in the middle of the situation.

Chances are you will not immediately know that information in the midst of conflict or painful situations. In most cases, once I've worked through them and some time has passed, I will discover that valuable information while reflecting on those past events. This helps me come to completion and resolve those issues fully.

When we see the soul's purpose in situations and resolve or come to peace with something that has happened, then our unresolved past issues are freed energetically. At this crucial life moment, we are transmuting the energy in our Akashic Field from negative to positive. This shift then affects our clarity in life and allows us to have our life path revealed in a deeper, more meaningful way.

Another interesting aspect of how we block ourselves in our interaction with the Akashic Field is the way we focus our awareness on duality or dualistic thinking. Thinking in terms of duality means that everything in our life becomes divided into opposites e.g. Good vs. Bad, Hate vs. Love,

Confined vs. Freedom, Energetic vs. Lazy, Light vs. Dark. We are all trapped in polarity. We all like things to be happy and perfect all the time but the reality is that sometimes, especially in our world with so much emphasis on duality, it will not be that way. Through our soul growth we are ultimately trying to release duality. Completion of our life lessons can evolve us toward oneness by resolving or transmuting unresolved energies contained in the Akashic Field.

For some reason, we typically prefer that *contrast* of *duality* when in essence all experiences are the same. In other words, it's an illusion that duality exists since all events blend into oneness when we become enlightened. Contrast means that for every experience we have there is a soul intention associated with it (what we are trying to learn) and often we choose the exact opposite (contrast) experience in order to learn it.

The energetic process of the Akashic Field is to resolve duality and allow us to transmute the negative energy we have created. When we clear up these energies, we release the field and move it from stagnant energy to an active quantum creating force in our lives.

Always remember that everything has a purpose or a meaning to it. When we are living our daily lives, those traumatic experiences happen in order for us to gain some awareness or insight that we couldn't see before. In other words, sometimes someone has to literally "shake our tree" for us to figure it out.

Here's an example of what I mean. I'll explain it using a very simple idea. What if our soul intention was to learn about courage? We could learn about courage in many different ways.

One way, could be to have an experience where someone was in trouble and we had to be courageous to help them. Another could be to experience an intense trauma or to become a victim in order to find the courage from within to overcome the situation. There can be a myriad of other reasons as well.

It may be helpful also to give a real example to illustrate how negative unresolved Akashic Field patterns can block positive potentials in your life. I have changed the name to remain confidential.

> *Janice is a yoga instructor who owns her own studio. She has been in business for over 10 years. She loves her students and enjoys the positive creation of a fulfilling career doing what her heart*

guides her to. Janice was one of the very first yoga studios' in the town where she lives.

Janice had a common business problem, lack of cash flow. She consulted marketing gurus, business advisors and others to help increase her exposure and hopefully help her attract more students.

For many years the results were up and down. Often it would become very stressful. She meditated on abundance a lot and tried everything she could spiritually to draw more abundance to the studio.

She wasn't even concerned with making a lot of money, just enough to insure she could continue to do the work to spread her love of yoga.

No matter what she did, the problem still remained. After putting so much energy into her work and becoming increasingly frustrated about her issues with lack of abundance she contacted me.

We turned to the Akashic Field to find out what patterns were stored that could prevent her from consciously creating abundance in her business. We uncovered several patterns that were contributing to the situation she was faced with.

In a past life experience she was in a religious community where part of her commitments was to take a vow of poverty. She had also taken a vow of sacrifice to be of service to others. These two vows were written into her Akashic Field so her subconscious continued to honor them despite her conscious efforts.

Other patterns were found. One was a replaying pattern of lack that was feeding into her subconscious all the time. This information kept her perception seeing only the lack in her life rather than the positive attributes. She also had a stored trauma of poverty that contributed to fears about not having enough money. All of these patterns together blocked the positive potentials for abundance in her life.

There are many ways that our unresolved soul memories can create various outcomes in our lives. For Janice several things were blocking her, not only the vow but also the fear of lack in her life. When we see our lives through our fears, we diminish our energy and ability to create positive things.

If you met Janice you wouldn't think she's particularly fearful of anything. Her subconscious was trying to protect her by averting away from unpleasant memories or helping to honor her previous vows. Her vow of sacrifice also meant that she had the belief that it was necessary to sacrifice herself for her work to the degree that she could not balance her own financial needs with the needs of her students.

After identifying these patterns and clearing them from her Akashic Field she was able to move through this up and down period of life with her business and create more balance and abundance with her heart's work.

I gave this example so that you can begin to see your life as a constant process of accessing your soul memories and utilizing at some level everything you've stored in the Akashic Field. If you look at your life and see repeating patterns, then most likely your higher self is attempting to get you to resolve certain issues to free the energies that need to be released.

Since the Akashic Field also stores every future possibility for us, unresolved issues can block our access to many of them because we are still using vast amounts of energy to resolve old patterns or create the repetition of life situations in order to get the information we need.

If we bury vast parts of ourselves or succumb to behaviors that allow us to run from our emotions, we can block the movement of vital energy substantially. Not facing whatever is needed, will cause a great deal of energy both emotionally and physically to be expended at a deep subconscious level to avoid unpleasant feelings.

If we work consciously to help free our unresolved patterns, then we can heal our past by transmuting our negative energy to positive potentials. As we release negative energies from the Akashic Field, we can expand our conscious perceptions of reality to allow for greater opportunities to create whatever we desire.

In order for you to begin working with the Akashic Field directly, you will need to discover the core issues that are blocking you. These core issues will help you identify the source of traumatic patterns you have left unresolved so you can release them.

Chapter Three
Recognizing Your Core Issues

"Resolve to find thyself;
and to know that
they who find themself,
lose their misery."

-- Matthew Arnold

The most challenging part of recognizing our core issues is that most of them are playing out very quickly in our subconscious mind and we can either deal with or suppress our subsequent emotions in various ways.

Some people are able to express emotions readily and others are not. Those that have difficulty may substitute other defenses such as anger in order to cover up how they are really feeling.

Over the past decade the world has gained many methods for creating greater self awareness and spiritual growth. This global awareness is fortunate. This new age of spiritual awareness has helped us to begin to see areas of our life that cause fear. We truly have a variety of tools available that can help us become better at confronting issues as they arise. With everything now available for working through emotional issues, it's important to know that working with the Akashic Field can be used to complement any of them.

Working with our core issues can be a slow process for many of us since we need to relearn often completely ingrained patterns of behavior that were learned. Perhaps your family ignored key issues or like my family used humor to cover up those "unspoken" problems we were having. We all got a great laugh, but very little of our emotional issues were ever completely resolved.

Over time we may learn to feel our emotions, but it's still hard to get at what caused them or the defensive reaction in the first place.

Healing our lives begins with our own conscious awareness of our issues. We have to work at identifying the internal thoughts and negative beliefs we have about ourselves first.

One of my favorite Latin phrases is, "*Temet Nosce*", which means "Know Thyself". The phrase was also made more notable by the popular *Matrix* movies.

I believe we must get to know ourselves in order to make better choices that can free us from the areas of our life where we are stuck and unable to grow.

We often hear a lot of suggestions from various writers and teachers about trying to "slow down" or "be present in the moment". This is especially challenging for each of us because we live in a time where our lives are complicated by financial stress, long work hours, dysfunctional relationships and the limited perceptions we have about what we really want and need to be happy.

I have learned over the years the huge benefit slowing down can make in my own life. I had to make a real effort to pay attention to my thoughts, beliefs and judgments. Being in the moment will allow you greater capability to work through whatever is emerging from your subconscious realm that needs to be dealt with and resolved. Only then can you recognize the self-imposed restrictions you have placed on yourself.

I used to hear these types of suggestions and think, okay that sounds like a good idea but how do I start doing that? During my own learning, I was given a great tool from my teacher. This tool became the best advice I had ever received. The tool I learned from my teacher was to *track my thoughts*. He asked me to become aware of whatever I was thinking throughout the day.

Tracking your thoughts, may seem hard a first, but over time it becomes easier. I have also learned that thoughts are not just our brains firing but are comprised of energy. This energy helps to create our life experiences.

Simply put, having positive thoughts results in more positive experiences and negative ones of course the reverse. It is our thoughts that are the key in everything that we do. This is an important fact because it is our thoughts that become transcribed onto the Akashic Field whether they are positive or negative.

Of our nearly 60,000 thoughts per day, our brains become conditioned for life based on our thoughts and experiences. Numerous studies have shown that our brain grows neural pathways in response to those experiences. Consequently if we have addictive habits, it will grow pathways to support them. If we have a lot of negative experiences it will grow those pathways that support our subconscious fears and so on. This is the physical aspect of our connection to the Akashic Field and its influence on us.

Our brains are constantly bombarded with sensory data. It puts this information into a conscious picture for us. To prevent information overload, the brain filters whatever it feels are extraneous bits of information. This process creates our reality from moment to moment.

If that's true then we are only consciously aware of a fraction of what is out there to become realized. Any information that comes through our conscious awareness is then shaped to conform to our values, beliefs, and other views. This can also mean that important information is simply filtered out if we have no frame of reference for it.

This point explains a common communication issue we can have with people in our lives. How often do you talk to someone and not feel as though they are listening and in some cases even heard you? Whatever you were sharing in that moment was filtered out because the persons' views wouldn't support additional conversation about the topic. Or perhaps their focus was on other things having nothing to do with what you shared. They could also be reacting subconsciously to unresolved soul memories.

One of my favorite stories to illustrate my point about our filters or what could be called our perception is about a tribal shaman in the early America's. This was a period of time when explorers were first journeying to America. I had heard this story many years ago. If you've seen the new movie, *What the Bleep...Do We Know?!?* Then you've already heard a similar version of this story:

> *One day a shaman was walking along the beach and looked out over the water. A huge ship was barely visible coming toward him. The shaman studies the water for a few minutes and even though the ship is there, he cannot see it in the water. The shaman had never seen a ship before in his entire life.*
>
> *Later that day he walks to the shore again and though he still cannot see the ship he stands there staring at the water. One of his tribesmen comes up to him and asks him what he's doing. The shaman points toward the direction of the ship and says he doesn't know but thinks something is out there.*
>
> *The next day the ship is even closer and the shaman returns. He can see that something is disturbing the water but still cannot actually see the ship. He continues to stare because he knows something should be there.*
>
> *The next day when he goes out to the water, he sees the huge ship off the coast. He calls everyone to the shore and points to the ship. He excitedly tries to show his tribes' people the strange object coming toward them. Not one of the others could see the ship.*

The other tribesmen couldn't see this massive ship of explorers coming because their brains filtered out the visual data since they had no idea what a ship even was. Since their brains had no correlation for a ship, it simply filtered out that information from what they were seeing. We can also filter out things that are deemed unimportant to us.

I can think of many times I have encountered lesser but somewhat similar experiences. Many times in my life, I can remember walking through my house of several years and suddenly notice something that I didn't even know was there. This has happened with light fixtures or other household items. I'm walking through a room and suddenly my attention focuses on it. I think, "Where did that come from?" It's not that the fixture simply appeared out of thin air; it had been there the whole time. Have you ever had that experience?

R A S

It's the same concept as the previous story of the shaman. Our brains continually filter out what it considers at the time unimportant information. Whatever is considered important or relevant to the moment is captured and considered by our conscious mind. Our subconscious defenses can also regulate whatever we focus on because of our emotions that can be triggered from information accessed in our soul memories.

Several years ago I was out with two very good friends. We were shopping and going out for lunch. During our outing, we witnessed a car accident while leaving a parking lot. It was a pretty typical accident. The person in front of me didn't watch carefully before pulling out onto a busy street. An oncoming car collided into the car that was pulling out. There was a man in the oncoming car and a woman in the car that pulled out in front of him. Thankfully no one was hurt.

The man got out of his car and was very angry. The lady looked shaken and was talking to him moving her arms wildly. They continued to argue until the police arrived.

Later that day we returned to my home. When we came in, my husband asked us if we had a good time while we were out. I started to tell him about the accident. My friends started filling in details of course but the interesting part was that both of their versions of what was seen were different than my own. There was a consensus that the accident occurred between the cars, but we differed on many finer points. One friend said the woman was heavy set, while I thought she was much thinner than described. I remember the man as being in his 50's and one friend said she thought he was much younger. There were other points of difference.

I was deeply impacted during that conversation because we were all there and saw the same thing but had very different stories to tell. How is that possible? Which of our three stories was true? Eventually in my own growth I figured out that they all were true. My friends and I had a different set of internal filters, so our experiences were similar but also different. This happens in our lives all the time. Each person's unique set of life experiences causes different perceptions of reality. Many times what is stored in our brains is not what really happened but our perception of what actually occurred. Much of this is driven by our subconscious as it gains access to soul memories.

Perhaps my one friend who saw the man as a teenager had experienced a past car accident and the person who hit her was a teenager. Perhaps the lady reminded my other friend of someone who was indeed similar but over weight. We make these types of correlations between similar objects or ideas all the time. The way our brain matches up information drives our perceptions of reality. We often do not see what we think we see.

We all experience fear in our daily lives. Our defense mechanisms are built around protecting us from whatever is perceived as a threat to our well-being. Remember that this is one of the basic functions of the subconscious. If we can learn to be conscious of our thoughts, it can allow us to over-ride our natural fear based responses and make different choices. It may not change our initial reaction to perceived threats but can help us to change some of the pathways that the brain has formed.

The key is to try and catch our thoughts so we can work with them. Initially, it overwhelmed me to consider catching a small portion of my approximately 60,000 thoughts per day. My teacher must have seen the look in my eyes. I was soon told that catching even one thought per day could start changes in my life. I gave it a try, remembering how a single word change had shifted my reality before. Just like my previous experience, it helped me tremendously open my awareness of my core issues.

Our thoughts determine the present and future of what is contained within our lives. It's all about *our* choices. How and what we choose, upon what we focus, concentrate, or direct our attention, and where we spend our mental and emotional energies – this is precisely what we will attract or draw to ourselves. And the universe *always* provides.

We all experience negative thoughts produced by fears every day at both a subconscious and conscious level. If our intent is to work with them, it will become easier and easier to try and shift them into more positive perceptions.

When I first started this process, I am sure I had hundreds of negative thoughts a day, and noticed very few of them. Trying to be conscious of them took a real effort at first. After awhile I noticed more and more of my negative thoughts when I was having them. From there I got to the point that I had less negative thoughts a day, and I noticed a lot of them.

Now I can catch my negative thoughts much more quickly and help myself out of these types of limited perceptions. The best thing to do when you have a negative thought is to acknowledge that you had one. Whether you realize it or not, you now have a choice to make about what you do with that information.

Most people do not realize that nothing has to be permanently stored as originally perceived. If that had not been pointed out to me by my teacher, I'm not sure I would have gained that awareness very easily.

Having negative thoughts is not the true problem, what we do with them is. We don't need to strive to eradicate all negative thoughts since it is part of being a human being. When I first embarked on a spiritual path, I thought I simply needed to eradicate all negative thoughts and move toward being more loving all the time in order to become "enlightened".

So I tried very hard to live that way. Since I was carrying unresolved issues, I would have negative experiences, behaviors and thoughts creep into my life. This made me become very upset when my own negativity would enter my awareness. I felt I was less than perfect and somehow flawed since I couldn't remain in a place of unconditional love. I often thought negative of myself for having these negative situations. You might easily see how this would run me in complete circles and create even more negativity. And it did.

I finally had to understand that I would have negative thoughts. There will be situations viewed as traumatic or undesirable. The important thing to remember is when you become aware of your negative thoughts <u>you</u> have the power to change them.

Every negative thought or experience can be transformed in one of two ways. First, the storyline can be mentally rewritten (called a content change). Second, the framework, structure or stage upon which the story takes place can be altered (called a context change).

For example, one day I was judging myself for making a mistake on a calculation in my checkbook. I thought to myself "CJ, you're so stupid". This information hit my conscious awareness by first noticing that I had the thought. I then told myself it was okay to have the negative thought about myself. I consciously looked at the reasons that proved the statement was not true. I thought about being a good parent, being very loving and being intelligent in various areas of my life. The final piece was changing the original thought by saying, "CJ you are not stupid. You are a wonderful person." Doing something like this is an example of using content change.

Transforming your negative thoughts allows you to imprint positive energy into the Akashic Field. You can take an active role in working with this field of energy by trying to complete the lesson, rather than leaving the imprinted energy as negative. This can be a very powerful tool in your every day life.

Here's another example showing there are always different ways to perceive situations in your life:

> You are sitting in traffic on your way home from work. It's been a long day. You have a lot to do when you arrive home. Fix some dinner, help your best friend clean out her garage and finish reading for a class you are taking.
>
> Traffic finally starts moving and you are glad to get going. Just as you accelerate, a car flies past you on the shoulder of the road and jumps into the line 6 cars ahead of you. It startles you first and then you get angry. "How dare that person jump in front of the line? I have been waiting here for quite awhile patiently. Why can't they just wait their turn like the rest of us?"
>
> Instantly your subconscious accesses your soul memories from your Akashic Field. Many patterns of imprinted energy begin to surface where you recall subconsciously a situation where you were disrespected. Another memory surfaces where you were harassed by someone. Suddenly your anger flies into a mixture of simultaneous feelings and reactions that are hard to separate. You feel hurt, sad, victimized and vulnerable.

You now have two choices regarding your situation. You can either be conscious of your true feelings in order to process and understand them. Or you can simply get angrier and lash out at the driver of the other car in blame.

If you choose in this situation to consider other possibilities for the haste of the other driver you may see more in the situation than you did before.

First of all, it's important to acknowledge that the driver's behavior has absolutely nothing to do with you. We all make other's actions very personal to ourselves when indeed they are not.

We are only personally responsible for our own actions and not those of other people even those close to us. If you remind yourself that the actions of the other driver were not meant to directly harm you personally, then you've made a context change.

You can consider that the person may have a reason to be hurrying. I do this often and find myself considering a wider array of possibilities - perhaps a family emergency, perhaps he or she is worried about something and cannot find out about it until they get to their destination. I can even go to more depth with this situation in my own awareness. I can think that he or she were there to remind me that I need to be patient or to learn something else. I can even pray that he or she will arrive at the destination without getting hurt.

This is a context change. It is a context change because you've changed your previous viewpoint of the situation to an entirely different one.

This information can be applied to all challenging life situations; the key is to consider other possibilities in life not just your first reaction and belief about it. It is perfectly okay to have your immediate reactions of fear or anger. Those emotions are real for you and generated from soul memories accessed by the subconscious mind. At first I found it hard to believe that we have the power to shift our thoughts and change them in the moment, but we do.

When we are able to use this tool in our lives, we are actively working with the Akashic Field to release unresolved issues and complete our soul growth opportunities.

You must known yourself at a greater depth and be willing to resolve and heal your past so you can consciously program your Akashic Field to express positive energy in your life.

This type of awareness will increase your ability to call positive quantum potentials into action without unnecessary subconscious blocks hindering what ever you are trying to create in your life.

Chapter 4

Common Blocking Patterns

"Let me not pray to be sheltered from dangers,
but to be fearless in facing them.

Let me not beg for the stilling of my pain,
but for the heart to conquer it."

- Rabindranath Tagore

It has been amazing to see so many similar patterns emerge for a majority of people during my client sessions. My healing method deals with thousands of stored patterns and combinations, but there are some core themes associated with many of them. It would be impossible to describe all possible patterns in this book. However, I can provide some of the most common ones and show you how to recognize if you have them in your Akashic Field.

These common themes are the way you can work with your own Akashic Field by recognizing them in yourself and then using the recommended affirmations to work through and release them. These affirmations are listed in the next chapter and were developed through my own research in private client sessions.

To assist you in identifying these patterns, I have provided examples of common ways these core issues can appear in your life. I hope this will help you really look at your life in a new way and see if you identify with any of the issues.

When reading each description, consciously open your mind to help you see them in your life. It may help to think of any challenging situations you may have at home, at work, with friends or family. Try to think of these as areas of resistance in your life where energy may be blocked.

If you identify with any core issue you read about here, then it may be a good affirmation to work with. If there are more than one, which would be perfectly normal, then start with the issue you most strongly identify with. If you are unsure where to begin, you can work with whatever you feel you should using your own intuition. You can also work with them all in order, one at a time.

All of these described issues have specific affirmations that were written to address and release old negative patterns and insert new positive aspects in their place.

Abandonment
This pattern type can be obvious or subtle. If you have fear of abandonment you may be a person who clings to relationships or may go out of your way to do things to keep someone from leaving your life. You could react in the reverse by avoiding close relationships to make sure that there isn't an opportunity for anyone to abandon you.

Abandonment patterns can generate many subconscious fears about relationships to others, trusting them or yourself and lower self-esteem.

Abuse

When you have patterns of physical or emotional abuse, it can generate all kinds of energy that can block you. This type of pattern can be present even if you haven't had abusive situations in your present life.

If your soul memories contain these patterns then you can have situations where you feel victimized by life. It is possible to have feelings of being attacked or react to an attack even when the other person isn't really attacking you.

If you are prone to a lot defensive reactions it could be this type of pattern. Another way this type of pattern can show up is having feelings of being unloved, unlovable, victimized, unsupported or unworthy.

Addiction

Addiction can show up in many ways other than the more obvious ones such as drugs or alcohol. We can become addicted to behaviors, addicted to people, addicted to stress and fear. If you have addiction patterns you, may have difficulty letting go of things or people and obsess about certain situations.

You may have a problem moving forward from the past and this can block you from creating your future. These patterns can create feelings of guilt, control, manipulation and shifting moods.

Anxiety

All of us can become anxious at different times in our lives. Patterns of anxiety can lead to needless worry over life situations and feeling unable to cope with whatever is happening. If you spend a lot of time concerning yourself with things you have no control over, then you may have anxiety patterns that are stored.

In addition to feelings of anxiety these patterns can cause intense feelings of hopelessness, of being unloved, of being incapable, and of sadness. If you identify with these patterns then overwhelmed patterns may be there as well.

Atonement

Most people don't recognize these patterns very easily. Atonement is a pattern when we feel that we have to atone or make up for past failures. This can affect how we balance our own needs with the needs of others.

We can fail to take care of ourselves in a loving way or consider what our real needs are. This type of pattern restricts people significantly because they are in a consistent state of offering retribution. This is a strong block because so much energy is channeled by a person in order to make retribution or atonement for something.

Other behaviors that can indicate atonement patterns can be tendencies to say you are sorry very often even when you have nothing to be sorry for. You can have feelings of extreme guilt and/or regret or a need to make up for past perceived failures.

You can also have situations in your life where no matter what you do you feel strongly that you cannot win and nothing you can do will ever make it right or that you are a failure.

Attachment

It is easy to be attached to people, places or things in our life such as a cup of coffee every morning or friends in our life. We can even become attached to our behaviors or reacting a certain ways. Some attachments can become severe enough to create addictions.

These types of patterns can also make it hard to let go of things, points of view or even a need to be right.

Betrayal

In our lives it can be hard not to feel betrayed at one time or another. These patterns can make us feel that those we trust will ultimately betray us. This can keep us locked in a survival mode rather than really living by keeping part of ourselves from being vulnerable or exposed. These patterns can block true emotional intimacy in our relationships.

If you have issues with trusting yourself or others these patterns may exist. Patterns of betrayal can make it difficult to have friends you really trust. The reverse can also be true and cause you to choose unhealthy friendships that are not worthy of your trust. This behavior is generated from a need to create betrayal in order to prove the belief you have in betrayal is true. Victim patterns may also be present with betrayal patterns.

Blame

These patterns can exist as either self-blame or blame of others. How often do you feel others are to blame for everything that you feel is wrong in your life?

Do you have feelings that everything wrong in your life or in others is your fault? Feelings of guilt or failure can be present with this type of pattern and cause you to feel responsible for others' sadness. Guilt is a similar pattern that may also be present.

Confinement

Patterns of confinement can sometimes appear in your life in very subtle ways. In order to identify patterns of confinement, you can look at the areas of your life where you hold yourself back.

Are you a person that focuses on the things you "should" do? If you get a great idea that will make you happy are there usually other thoughts that follow it where you can tell yourself why you can't?

Confinement has feelings of being stuck, restricted or prevented from doing what you want. You may feel that other's wishes are far more important than your own. You may also choose relationships where the other person is allowed to control your actions or where your power is given away.

Control

This can be a tricky one to spot especially since control can be a way of avoiding emotions that are unpleasant. Our ego tries convincing us that we have the ability to control ourselves or others, but we don't.

This type of control is really an illusion. Are you a person that must plan everything out to the finest detail? Do you feel angry when things don't go according to plan? How comfortable are you with change? Do you force yourself to do things a particular way even when there are other options or do you expect other to do them that way?

Control patterns can stifle or block spiritual energy and our connection to our higher self and inner wisdom.

Denial
Accepting life as it comes can be difficult to do. Denial patterns exist when trauma makes us feel that we cannot face the reality of painful situations so ignoring their existence is the only way to cope.

People with denial patterns often have a lot of trauma stored in their Akashic Field. Clearing these patterns can bring greater acceptance for life.

Disappointment
We all know there are disappointments in life but what if life was just a huge disappointment to you? Disappointment patterns can make it hard to feel that things will go the way you want them to.

They can create fears about new situations and opportunities because of the subconscious belief that you will eventually feel disappointed. This can affect your friendships, relationships and your quality of life.

If you expect the worst then often you get exactly what you expected. Releasing these patterns can remove blocks to happiness.

Distrust
Distrust can keep you separated from other people in your life. Distrust patterns can also relate to you. Do you often second guess the decisions you make? Do you find it very difficult or nearly impossible for you to make a decision?

When you have distrust for others, then it may be hard for you to believe in good outcomes will happen in your life. You may also have distrust for life itself with the belief that nothing will go well for you no matter what you do. This belief is similar to patterns of suffering.

Failure
Those with failure patterns feel like a failure even when they are successful. It can be difficult for them to feel successful at any aspects of life.

Traumatic past situations and feelings of failure cause this belief to be stored and block possible life successes. This can also block you from being able to reach new goals or cause you to procrastinate due to fear of failure. Fear of failure can permeate beliefs in all life areas: relationships, career, spirituality and others.

Guilt
Guilt can be some of the heavier patterns stored in the Akashic Field. Guilt can cause a lot of different behaviors in your life. Feeling guilty can tie up a lot of energy as you subconsciously try to make up for whatever you feel you did wrong.

These patterns can affect how you react to situations that happen and blame yourself for negative outcomes. Do you often say "sorry" for little things even when you were not to blame?

Isolation
Another word for isolation can be separation though both patterns have distinct differences. These patterns can make you feel disconnected from others or not a part of the crowd for no apparent reason. Feelings of loneliness can be a part of this pattern.

Persons with these patterns can be challenged in relationships even if they want them because they subconsciously feel they are not connected to others. Isolation can also cause feelings of not being able to rely on others when it's most important.

Lack
People who focus on what they do not have in their life can have this pattern type. Lack can also affect areas of abundance in all areas of life: relationships, career or spirituality. Lack patterns can make it difficult to balance finances or manifest prosperity as well.

People with these patterns can have related poverty consciousness. This can also create fears of lack even in the presence of abundance.

Loss
Feelings of loss can affect our lives tremendously. Whether we have lost a loved one, a prized possession, livelihood, money or other important aspect in our lives it can take along time to resolve the sadness, hurt and pain.

Unresolved loss can block energy for many years or even lifetimes. If you have loss patterns, you may worry needlessly about losing something or someone. Other unexplained sadness, greater difficulty healing any type of loss in your life may be symptoms of loss patterns. Having tremendous fear about losing things in your life, may reflect unresolved loss.

Negativity

People with these patterns can have a difficult time looking on the brighter side even if they are trying consciously to do so. It can be experienced like a negative voice playing over and over again.

This can be a frustrating pattern when trying to embrace growth and change because it can cause negative thoughts and feelings to surface when you are consciously trying to see all things as positive experiences.

Resolving negativity and old negative thought forms can help to achieve greater balance spiritually and create the open opportunity for growth.

Overwhelmed

These patterns deal with those times in life when we feel incapable of doing whatever we must do. This type of pattern has feelings of life spiraling out of control.

Overwhelmed patterns can show up as becoming more easily distracted especially if there is a lot going on in your life which is either avoidance or subconscious procrastination. This has to do with the subconscious belief that you lack the capability to successfully take care of whatever is necessary so you avoid the possibility of failure.

Sacrifice

Continual self-sacrifice is the key hallmark of this pattern type. Giving of ourselves to others is not a negative behavior but in this pattern there is an extreme tendency to become unbalanced between others needs and our own needs.

Patterns of sacrifice lead to imbalance in the energies of our life and create an inability to give much to ourselves even when truly needed. Sacrifice patterns come from soul memories or situations where we feel we must give all of ourselves to cope with a situation. They can also be generated from past life religious vows or commitments.

Separation
How often do we feel lonely in our lives? Separateness from others is the sense that you are on you own in life and have been harshly judged by others. We all need to feel connected in life to our families, friends, communities and the world. When we lack that connectedness it can be that we have patterns of separation in place. The belief that we are separate can have a profound impact on the richness of our relationships and our feelings of well-being.

Previous life experiences of exile or being cast out of our community or family unit can create intense patterns of separation in our Akashic Field.

Suffering
Past traumas can create the belief in suffering as an inherent part of life experience. These emotional or physical challenges can solidify subconscious beliefs that all of life requires suffering. There is also the belief that anything good we can achieve in life must come through our suffering.

A subtle way this can show up is as a lack of worthiness. Feelings of not being worth much or worthy of good things can be present. These patterns can make life hard all the time or make it feel like a burden. Multiple patterns of suffering can rob the joy and happiness from life and create suppressed anger.

Victim
Stored trauma associated from abusive situations causes patterns of victimization. Victim patterns often recreate from lifetime to lifetime even if the originating situation was started in another past life experience.

People with these patterns feel weaker at coping with life at times. They often feel like they are a victim in their life. They feel powerless to do anything about it and thus do not confront many issues with others.

This type of pattern can also create an emotional addiction to play the role of victim either by using victimization as a method of taking less accountability, manipulating others or by choosing situations to further the belief that they will be victimized by others.

Chapter Five

Rewrite Your Akashic Field

"Each morning we are born again.
What we do today is what matters most."

-Buddha

Rewriting the Akashic Field is an energetic process that can be initiated by anyone. Many people ask me, "How is it possible to re-write my Akashic Field?" My answer is simply this, "It is your energy. Your thoughts determine what is recorded into your Akashic Field. Your conscious choices can rewrite the field the same way."

It is your choices that determine what is resolved or unresolved. It is inherently simple with intention, directed energy and specific information to re-write your Akashic Field.

We all have negative energy in our Akashic Field. How much we are willing to look at our issues and resolve them determines how much will remain unresolved. Your unresolved issues become the barriers you may have to reaching the goals of what you want in your life.

The affirmations in the book give you some possible tools for releasing negative behaviors or past traumas and imprinting positive energies in their place.

Our journey through life is full of a variety of experiences designed for the specific purpose of growth and evolution. Whenever we learn something new or revisit what has happened and are able to change what we previously believed about it, we are essentially rewriting our past. Doing so allows the energy in the Akashic Field to shift and clear in a tremendous way. It is important as a people we learn to view various life situations that we perceive as negative in a different way.

As we learn and grow we are changing our Akashic Field and opening more available spiritual resources. We are essentially raising the abundance of positive energies that are available to us. When we choose to open to new possibilities or different perceptions, we are engaging the most powerful quantum energy we have at our disposal. I have seen tremendous growth happen very quickly for myself, friends and clients.

All the positive choices that you're making in your life directly affect the balance of positive and negative energies in your Akashic Field. More positive viewpoints allow you to create more positive in your life. The reverse is also true.

That is why working with your thoughts can help you change your life. All of the things discussed in this book can help to set quantum energy into motion. Whenever you are trying to heal your life, you're energetically rewriting your Akashic Field.

In order to use this book there is a process that will allow you to direct your energy and intention toward the Akashic Field to release past traumas, negative energy or unhealthy patterns of behavior.

Here is a 4-step process for accessing your Akashic Field and using the affirmations in this book to clear negative patterns:

Step 1-- *Create The Proper Intention*

We all have the power to focus and use directed energy in the form of our intention. Since the Akashic Field is imprinted with our thoughts, we can use "stronger thoughts" to direct what is released or imprinted to it.

To be effective, it is important that you properly align your intention for the purpose of using the affirmations. Don't concern yourself with whether or not you can access the Akashic Field properly because is as easy as a thought to do so. Anyone can do this work.

You can relax any doubting thoughts you have about your effectiveness since it is really impossible with your conscious intention to not access the Akashic Field correctly.

Aligning yourself with proper intention is simply your way of focusing your attention toward what you are doing.

You can easily set your intention before beginning by insuring your subconscious; conscious and super-conscious (high self) are connected.

You can say the following in order to do so:

I AM Divine. I AM Unconditional Love. I AM fully connected to universal energies. I request that my subconscious, conscious and super-conscious (high self) be connected. May I have full access to my Akashic Field for the purpose of this work today, thank you.

Feel free to substitute your own words that are similar in focus. You may also use whatever you feel connects you to universal energies and will allow you to bring forth whatever is in your highest good.

Step 2--*Generating spiritual energy for your affirmation*

Each of us possesses life force or vital energy, also referred to as "chi", "prana" or simply "spiritual energy." In order to release limiting energies from the Akashic Field and imprint positive ones using the affirmations, you need to consciously generate enough spiritual energy to help them work more effectively. If you skip this step, you will still access the Akashic Field, but the results will not be as powerful.

Many ancient cultures consider breath the best way to create life force energy. Many physical and spiritual practices available today incorporate breath such as yoga. Bio-feedback and other relaxation techniques using deep breathing can help to reduce stress, quiet our minds and other amazing benefits.

Try paying attention to how you are breathing during the day, is it shallow or do you stop breathing during stressful situations? Stress can affect your breathing rate. Taking some precious time to breathe deeply can help you to relax and let go of stress.

I remember practicing for a day to try and be mindful of my breath. I often caught myself holding my breath. I was doing this unconsciously a lot of the time. I have learned over time to breathe more deeply in order to have greater access to my own spiritual energy.

Vital force or spiritual energy is actually created by deep breathing because it causes our bodies to begin burning blood sugar. We apply this same idea to generating the spiritual energy needed for these affirmations. Doing this technique also helps you to balance your brain wave patterns.

Do the following to generate spiritual energy:

1. Inhale for 7 counts (counting fairly rapidly)
2. Hold the breath for 1 count
3. Exhale for 7 counts

Repeat this process 3 times

As you do this deep breathing technique try to visualize your breath creating a ball of white light as you exhale that you will direct toward the Akashic Field during Step 3.

Step 3-- ***Directing Spiritual Energy into the Akashic Field***

After you've created proper intent and generated some spiritual energy, it's time to direct it in order to benefit your affirmation practice. Your subconscious mind already has the direct link to your Akashic Field.

You will now direct the spiritual energy you've created toward your subconscious mind and your Akashic Field. It is very beneficial to do this direction out loud for your subconscious to hear your request.

The following can be said aloud to direct the spiritual energy.

> *I request that the spiritual energy I have created be directed to my subconscious and Akashic Field for the purposes of my affirmation today.*

Step 4-- ***Select Your Affirmation***

When you select your first affirmation to work with, you will most likely have one of two possible intentions:

> *One*, to help heal a past unresolved issue you are aware of,
>
> or
>
> *Two*, to generate more positive spiritual energy & awareness.

Chapter 4 helps identify core issues and Chapter 6 shows affirmations that can be used for each issue. Chapter 7 are those affirmations for generating more positive spiritual growth.

Once you've completed this final step you are ready to begin working with your chosen affirmation.

Chapter Six

Affirmations for Healing the Past

"...Nothing is so healing as the
realization that he has
come upon the right word."

-Catherine Bowen

This chapter of the book contains the affirmations you can use for each core issue that you've identified.

Each affirmation is designed to help you gain access to the Akashic Field and release or heal certain negative patterns or subconscious blocks.

Ideally these affirmations should be used for 21 days in a row. If you skip a day, you should start your count over again. Don't worry too much if you have to start again; you are always receiving benefit from doing them. You wouldn't be the only person in the world that had to start more than one time to finish the recommended 21 days.

Many clients have asked me about the value of using an affirmation for a full 21 days. Though I'd like to take credit for the magical number 21, I can't.

Doing anything consistently for at least 21 days is particularly effective for changing various behaviors. This theory is based on various behavioral experts who have determined that it takes a minimum of 21 days for a new behavior to become a habit.

If you find working over a shorter period is easier for you, such as 10-14 days, then please do so. You should always trust yourself on what is best for you.

The most important point is to use them on a consistent basis in order to clear your unresolved issues from your Akashic Field. They will help if used for less than 21 days but may not as effective if they were.

If you are a person that is comfortable with a routine, it is okay to use them longer than the recommended 21 days since that is only the minimum target duration.

You can locate the affirmations you most identify and work with them one after another. You can also work with several at the same time.

At some level, all of the core issues represented in this book are somewhere in everyone's Akashic Field so you could work with each one and go through the entire list one at a time.

I recommend reading through the descriptions found in the previous chapter and then follow your heart to the first one that you identify with most and begin there.

For your convenience a personal notes page is located on the page across from each affirmation so that you can jot down dates to keep track or any new personal awareness you may gain during their use.

I often recommend that you use a pencil to write the date you start and each day you do the affirmation so you can keep track. If you have to start again this makes it easier to erase your dates.

You can also jot down any insights or realizations you have during the course of your use of the affirmation. If you like to write, I highly recommend starting an Akashic Field journal in a notebook for more lengthy writing about the insights you gain during your work with them.

While releasing your patterns and blocks, you will also be reinforcing positive new patterns. Each affirmation has been specifically created to address key patterns found represented a majority of the time in the core issues demonstrated during my client sessions.

Many of these affirmations were actually used as client "homework" following a private session. Others were written specifically for this book to release core issues and replace them with positive views or intentions.

The next section shows all available affirmations for each core issue I've explained and their corresponding page number for easier access.

The chart below shows the core issues described at length in the previous chapter with their corresponding affirmation and page number.

Primary Issue	***Affirmation Name***	***Page #***
Abandonment	Abandonment & Neglect	**61**
Abuse	Forgiveness of Self Forgiveness of Others	**63** **65**
Addiction	Freedom from Addictions	**67**
Anxiety	Releasing Worry	**69**
Atonement	Releasing Self Blame	**71**
Attachment	Letting Go of Attachments	**73**
Betrayal	Transformation of Anger	**75**
Blame	Living in Non-Judgment	**77**
Confinement	Embracing Freedom	**79**
Control	Letting Go of Control	**81**
Denial	Acceptance of Life	**83**
Disappointment	Healing Disappointment	**85**
Distrust	Greater Trust of Self and Others	**87**
Failure	Acknowledging Your Successes	**89**
Guilt	Releasing Guilt and Shame	**91**
Isolation	Greater Connection to Others	**93**
Lack	Manifesting Abundance	**95**
Loss	Healing & Overcoming Grief	**97**
Negativity	Increasing Positive Perception	**99**
Overwhelmed	Increasing Belief in Being Capable	**101**
Sacrifice	Open your Ability to Receive	**103**
Suffering	Ending Belief in Suffering	**105**
Victim	Healing Past Hurts Increasing Personal Responsibility	**107** **109**

Abandonment & Neglect

Instructions:
Create the proper intention in your mind (pg. 54). Do the breathing technique to generate spiritual energy (pg. 55). Say out loud before beginning: "I now gain access to my Akashic Field. I send the spiritual energy I have created to my Akashic Field for the purpose of the following affirmation."

Visualize the words as you express them out loud:

I am a child of the divine. I am given sustenance and am cherished by the divine each day which is my inheritance from the source of things.

I acknowledge my painful soul memories of abandonment. I know that those who I felt abandoned by were not able to give me what I felt I needed at that time.

This is not a reflection on my worthiness to receive love.

I truly know that I can provide myself with the sustenance I need instead of looking to others to give this to me.

I wish to heal my deep sadness and the fear I have that the situation was my fault. I know now that everything that happens is for a divine reason even if I am unable to see it.

I know am never truly abandoned and will allow nourishment in my life on all levels in order to participate in the growth and expansion I came into this world to complete.

I give my gifts freely and completely to myself and others. I create my own sustenance by my love for myself and all living things.

Thank you, Thank you, Thank you and So Let It Be.

(Take a final deep breath and release it completing your intention)

Personal Affirmation Notes

(Use this space to record your thoughts, feelings and experiences.)

Forgiveness of Self

Instructions:
Create the proper intention in your mind (pg. 54). Do the breathing technique to generate spiritual energy (pg. 55). Say out loud before beginning: "I now gain access to my Akashic Field. I send the spiritual energy I have created to my Akashic Field for the purpose of the following affirmation."

Visualize the words as you express them out loud:

I accept all my actions in the world as perfect and right for the given moment. I recognize that all situations and experiences are in my highest good.

I ask for healing in the areas of my life where I have judged myself for making choices I felt were best at the time but had a negative outcome for others.

I realize that I must take care of myself in all ways and follow my heart and inner wisdom to guide me.

I forgive and release myself from anxiety, self-limitations, guilt and other non-loving judgments regarding my value to others and my responsibilities in my life.

As I release my intention today, I honor my true self and request balanced responsibility and wisdom in my life to hear, know and embrace that which is mine to do.

No more and no less.

Thank you, Thank you, Thank you and So Let It Be.

(Take a final deep breath and release it completing your intention)

Personal Affirmation Notes

(Use this space to record your thoughts, feelings and experiences.)

Forgiveness of Others

Instructions:
Create the proper intention in your mind (pg. 54). Do the breathing technique to generate spiritual energy (pg. 55). Say out loud before beginning: "I now gain access to my Akashic Field. I send the spiritual energy I have created to my Akashic Field for the purpose of the following affirmation."

Visualize the words as you express them out loud:

I ask for healing in the areas of my life where I have judged others for making choices I felt were wrong and had a negative outcome for me.

I realize that all events in my life work for greater good even if I am unable to see the purpose. I trust in the process of my life.

I choose to forgive others and release the anger I am holding for whatever they have done.

Holding the anger and resentment only harms me and causes me to suppress myself in numerous ways.

I ask for greater wisdom to feel my emotions and resolve them fully and completely.

I set my daily intention to embrace the compassion necessary to grant forgiveness for those who have hurt me in all my life situations.

I request the wisdom to react in authenticity in my life situations.

I move forward lighter and freer of my anger and more open to receive the healing and guidance available from universal energies.

I accept my life and accept all persons as part of my growth, learning and understanding even in areas of conflict and resistance.

Thank you, Thank you, Thank you and So Let It Be.

(Take a final deep breath and release it completing your intention)

Personal Affirmation Notes

(Use this space to record your thoughts, feelings and experiences.)

Freedom from Addictions

Instructions:
Create the proper intention in your mind (pg. 54). Do the breathing technique to generate spiritual energy (pg. 55). Say out loud before beginning: "I now gain access to my Akashic Field. I send the spiritual energy I have created to my Akashic Field for the purpose of the following affirmation."

Visualize the words as you express them out loud:

I ask for the release of those areas of my life where I am controlled by my addictions to behaviors, people, objects or substances.

I realize this control is an illusion and that breaking this illusion will take time.

I ask for the liberation of the originating painful memories and situations that contributed to my release of power to my addictions. I desire to see the root of these issues and begin to work through them in a loving way toward myself and others.

I visualize and see myself with the inherent divine power to shift my energy from that of addiction and control to balance and wisdom.

I choose to love myself and see myself in freedom to grow and encompass my true nature in wisdom and compassion.

I ask for the ability to see that which is necessary in my life to free myself from addictive patterns. I ask for the wisdom to ask for help when needed and to open myself to healing energies of the universe.

I choose to breathe deeply when faced with difficult choices and to love myself even when I falter from my goals.

I surround myself and open to receive healing energies at all levels.

Thank you, Thank you, Thank you and So Let It Be.

(Take a final deep breath and release it completing your intention)

Personal Affirmation Notes

(Use this space to record your thoughts, feelings and experiences.)

Releasing Worry

Instructions:
Create the proper intention in your mind (pg. 54). Do the breathing technique to generate spiritual energy (pg. 55). Say out loud before beginning: "I now gain access to my Akashic Field. I send the spiritual energy I have created to my Akashic Field for the purpose of the following affirmation."

Visualize the words as you express them out loud:

I acknowledge the anxiety and worry that I have regarding the events in my life. I sometimes fear the unknown and this contributes to my discomfort each day.

I choose to accept the events of my life and relax my need to know what will happen next or to know the outcomes of my life choices.

I trust myself to make choices that are in my highest good and see the perfection of each life situation.

I see myself each day embracing a greater allowance for life to create as it's intended to.

I move forward lighter and freer of my anxiety and more open to receive the healing and guidance available from universal energies.

I accept my life and accept all persons as part of my growth, learning. I allow myself to gain greater understanding of my soul's purpose, even in areas that are full of unknowns.

I choose to be filled with peace each day knowing that the universe supports who I truly am and whatever purposes I have in my life.

Thank you, Thank you, Thank you and So Let It Be.

(Take a final deep breath and release it completing your intention)

Personal Affirmation Notes

(Use this space to record your thoughts, feelings and experiences.)

Releasing Self Blame

Instructions:
Create the proper intention in your mind (pg. 54). Do the breathing technique to generate spiritual energy (pg. 55). Say out loud before beginning: "I now gain access to my Akashic Field. I send the spiritual energy I have created to my Akashic Field for the purpose of the following affirmation."

Visualize the words as you express them out loud:

In the past I have blamed myself as the cause of others suffering. I have attempted through my actions to make up for my past perceived wrongs.

I have felt sorry for and blamed myself for situations that were not my responsibility and have carried this tremendous weight on my shoulders.

I am ready to be freed from this burden. I realize that I do not need to carry the weight of atonement.

I do not need to continuously blame myself for all my actions or spend unbalanced energy feeling guilt and blame.

I choose to accept myself and show compassion for myself in all areas of my life.

I choose to open myself to greater possibilities in my life and accept balanced responsibility in my life.

I accept my choices as right and perfect for myself and others. I realize that my life is filled with opportunities to grow and experience life in order to learn.

Thank you, Thank you, Thank you and So Let It Be.

(Take a final deep breath and release it completing your intention)

Personal Affirmation Notes

(Use this space to record your thoughts, feelings and experiences.)

<u>Letting Go of Attachments</u>

Instructions:

Create the proper intention in your mind (pg. 54). Do the breathing technique to generate spiritual energy (pg. 55). Say out loud before beginning: "I now gain access to my Akashic Field. I send the spiritual energy I have created to my Akashic Field for the purpose of the following affirmation."

Visualize the words as you express them out loud:

I acknowledge the areas of my life where I have unhealthy attachments. I desire to see all those attachments that have not been revealed to me yet.

I hold onto things in an unhealthy way due to fear of loss or pain. I choose to gain greater acceptance of all the circumstances of my life.

I choose now to allow the situations in my life to unfold for the greatest good for myself or others without having the need to become attached.

I am free from attachments with the knowledge and divine wisdom that all events in my life are created in order to promote growth and learning.

Freedom from my attachments will allow me to follow the best path for me in my life.

I can now choose letting go rather than holding on.

Thank you, Thank you, Thank you and So Let It Be.

(Take a final deep breath and release it completing your intention)

Personal Affirmation Notes

(Use this space to record your thoughts, feelings and experiences.)

Transformation of Anger

Instructions:
Create the proper intention in your mind (pg. 54). Do the breathing technique to generate spiritual energy (pg. 55). Say out loud before beginning: "I now gain access to my Akashic Field. I send the spiritual energy I have created to my Akashic Field for the purpose of the following affirmation."

Visualize the words as you express them out loud:

I acknowledge the toxicity my anger has in all areas of my life. I have been a prisoner to my anger for too long.

I realize knowing forgiveness would release the pain in my heart and allow me to heal the past. Making this choice will create a better future for myself and others in my life.

I know that anger is a part of my life. I accept that sometimes I will become angry at people or the events in my life.

I realize that holding onto anger is a choice, and I want to make more healthy choices in the future.

I ask for the transformation of my anger into divine love and for wisdom to learn from all my life experiences.

I ask for the future opportunities to resolve my past conflicts and unresolved feelings toward others and areas of my life that are out of control.

I move forward in greater acceptance of my life and choose to see each situation as a growth opportunity.

I grant myself love, compassion, non-judgment and wisdom so that I may share those energies with others in my life.

Thank you, Thank you, Thank you and So Let It Be.

(Take a final deep breath and release it completing your intention)

Personal Affirmation Notes

(Use this space to record your thoughts, feelings and experiences.)

Living in Non-Judgment

Instructions:
Create the proper intention in your mind (pg. 54). Do the breathing technique to generate spiritual energy (pg. 55). Say out loud before beginning: "I now gain access to my Akashic Field. I send the spiritual energy I have created to my Akashic Field for the purpose of the following affirmation."

Visualize the words as you express them out loud:

I ask for healing in the areas of my life where I have judged others for making choices that had a negative outcome for me.

Living in non-judgment means that I choose to view the world around me without my own expectations. I desire to live in trust and acceptance of the divine flow of life.

I choose to stop blaming others for whatever I believe is going wrong in my life. I acknowledge that all life situations are in my highest good.

I open my heart to create greater compassion, understanding and acceptance for others around me.

I ask for healing in those areas of my life where I have judged myself harshly. I know that every life circumstance is ultimately for my growth. I choose to allow myself the room to grow.

I release all my judgments of others and myself. I choose greater love for all things.

I know that I am capable of living in non-judgment and make my future choices accordingly.

Thank you, Thank you, Thank you and So Let It Be.

(Take a final deep breath and release it completing your intention)

Personal Affirmation Notes

(Use this space to record your thoughts, feelings and experiences.)

Embracing Freedom

Instructions:
Create the proper intention in your mind (pg. 54). Do the breathing technique to generate spiritual energy (pg. 55). Say out loud before beginning: "I now gain access to my Akashic Field. I send the spiritual energy I have created to my Akashic Field for the purpose of the following affirmation."

Visualize the words as you express them out loud:

I have experienced many restrictions in my life that have held me back and blocked my ability to grow and expand my self awareness.

My past patterns of confinement do not work for me and create unnecessary fears and discord. I choose to gently release those fears that bind me in all areas of my life.

Choosing freedom allows me to become who I truly am and to follow my heart's desires toward a happier life filled with joy and peace.

To know freedom is to move forward in my life with unlimited potential for growth and understanding.

I wish to fly free and embrace life without fears that can prevent me from seeing all the infinite possibilities that are available to me.

My past no longer has the control to prevent me from creating the life that I desire. I am free to play and create a reality that can stretch as far as my imagination.

I am creator in my life and desire happiness and joy. I feel freedom coursing through my entire body and allow positive energies to permeate my life.

I am like a spiritual bird flowing through life with greater ease and infinite beauty.

Thank you, Thank you, Thank you and So Let It Be.

(Take a final deep breath and release it completing your intention)

Personal Affirmation Notes

(Use this space to record your thoughts, feelings and experiences.)

Letting Go of Control

Instructions:
Create the proper intention in your mind (pg. 54). Do the breathing technique to generate spiritual energy (pg. 55). Say out loud before beginning: "I now gain access to my Akashic Field. I send the spiritual energy I have created to my Akashic Field for the purpose of the following affirmation."

Visualize the words as you express them out loud:

I visualize my fear as a dark cloud that covers my life and prevents the full expression of who I really am.

I understand that fear is what drives my need to control myself, others or life situations. My control is my way of feeling more comfortable, but I know this is only a temporary solution.

I choose to gradually let go of my need to control my surroundings. I desire to use to my energy in a different way in my life. I want to expand myself in a healthy way that will allow me to free myself to new and better circumstances.

I ask for the courage imprinted to allow my fears to be released. I ask for greater acceptance of life and trust that all situations work for my higher good.

I ask for universal energies to surround me and assist me when necessary. I open myself and am worthy to receive fully these gifts of spirit.

I grant myself healing at all levels to become that which I came into life to become. I desire to learn all that is available to me. I desire to share my love with myself and others in a deep and meaningful way.

I trust myself. I trust others. I trust my life to give me exactly what I need.

I am divine. I am love. I am always connected to my inner knowing.

Thank you, Thank you, Thank you and So Let It Be.

(Take a final deep breath and release it completing your intention)

Personal Affirmation Notes

(Use this space to record your thoughts, feelings and experiences.)

Acceptance of Life

Instructions:
Create the proper intention in your mind (pg. 54). Do the breathing technique to generate spiritual energy (pg. 55). Say out loud before beginning: "I now gain access to my Akashic Field. I send the spiritual energy I have created to my Akashic Field for the purpose of the following affirmation."

Visualize the words as you express them out loud:

I desire to live in greater acceptance of life and release my denial of the truth in my life situations.

It is my intention to let go of my fear of facing whatever I need to in order to grow in my life.

I ask for courage to resolve those patterns that prevent me from greater acceptance in my life.

I choose to accept myself, others, and situations. I trust that all parts of my life work together for greater good. I desire to learn all that I came to learn and do all that I intended to do.

I realize to reach my life path I must choose acceptance in my life rather than denial.

I see my divine nature in my life and am anxious to watch it unfold when I release control and allow manifestation of whatever is in my highest good.

Thank you, Thank you, Thank you and So Let It Be.

(Take a final deep breath and release it completing your intention)

Personal Affirmation Notes

(Use this space to record your thoughts, feelings and experiences.)

Healing Disappointment

Instructions:
Create the proper intention in your mind (pg. 54). Do the breathing technique to generate spiritual energy (pg. 55). Say out loud before beginning: "I now gain access to my Akashic Field. I send the spiritual energy I have created to my Akashic Field for the purpose of the following affirmation."

Visualize the words as you express them out loud:

I acknowledge my belief that life is about being disappointed.

In the past I have seen and expected to be disappointed by others in my life. This has set a very low expectation of the quality my life will be.

I choose to have a greater quality of life now. I do realize that I deserve more balance and happiness in my life.

I ask for the release of all my patterns that keep me from accepting life situations as working for my greater good. Some of these may be loss, hurt, betrayal, mistrust and abandonment.

I choose acceptance now and embrace a broader path for myself.
I ask to see the areas of my life now that I have a subconscious expectation of disappointment so I can work through these issues and resolve them.

I ask for wisdom to see the divine nature of all my life situations so that I may release disappointment and embrace growth and understanding.

I accept that life will have disappointments but that does not mean that my life will be a continual disappointment. I will not become stuck in this illusion any longer.

Thank you, Thank you, Thank you and So Let It Be.

(Take a final deep breath and release it completing your intention)

Personal Affirmation Notes

(Use this space to record your thoughts, feelings and experiences.)

Greater Trust of Self and Others

Instructions:
Create the proper intention in your mind (pg. 54). Do the breathing technique to generate spiritual energy (pg. 55). Say out loud before beginning: "I now gain access to my Akashic Field. I send the spiritual energy I have created to my Akashic Field for the purpose of the following affirmation."

Visualize the words as you express them out loud:

I see my pain in trusting myself and others as a thing of my past that I'd like to move pass now.

I send the energy of healing to my Akashic Field and ask for the liberation of those patterns that keep my distrusting behaviors in place as a defense mechanism in my life.

I choose to allow for trust to become a part of my life and also divine discernment to protect me from situations that are not good for me.

I see myself accessing my own divine wisdom and knowing whatever I need to do. I trust myself now to make choices in my highest good.

I can see myself open to the ability to see and know where trust should be given to others and where trust should not.

Ultimately I must love myself unconditionally in order to trust myself to know what I need to in order to be open and grow. I choose to allow for trust at greater levels in my life.

I ask for areas where my distrusting patterns come into play so that I may work through those issues in greater ease and understanding.

I can trust myself and open to receive divine healing in all areas of my life.

Thank you, Thank you, Thank you and So Let It Be.

(Take a final deep breath and release it completing your intention)

Personal Affirmation Notes

(Use this space to record your thoughts, feelings and experiences.)

Acknowledging Your Successes

Instructions:
Create the proper intention in your mind (pg. 54). Do the breathing technique to generate spiritual energy (pg. 55). Say out loud before beginning: "I now gain access to my Akashic Field. I send the spiritual energy I have created to my Akashic Field for the purpose of the following affirmation."

Visualize the words as you express them out loud:

I acknowledge the past parts of my life where I felt limited by feeling unsuccessful at manifesting my true purpose in life. I know that I am not a failure though at times I have felt this way.

I visualize and see all of my previously blocked energies regarding my own manifestation of successful feelings. I realize that all I have done works for greater good in my life and there are no failures, only learning opportunities.

I accept healing at all areas of my life where I limit myself and my divine potential.

I desire to be unlimited in the areas of personal and spiritual success. I now allow myself to manifest whatever I truly need and accept those miracles that happen as my highest good.

I see my life free and full of success at all levels.

I am ready to receive all the gifts from the divine returning to me in my world through unconditional love and compassion.

Thank you, Thank you, Thank you and So Let It Be.

(Take a final deep breath and release it completing your intention)

Personal Affirmation Notes

(Use this space to record your thoughts, feelings and experiences.)

Releasing Guilt and Shame

Instructions:
Create the proper intention in your mind (pg. 54). Do the breathing technique to generate spiritual energy (pg. 55). Say out loud before beginning: "I now gain access to my Akashic Field. I send the spiritual energy I have created to my Akashic Field for the purpose of the following affirmation."

Visualize the words as you express them out loud:

I know that I am worthy to receive abundant gifts in all areas of my life. I believe I deserve happiness.

I acknowledge that all life situations and experiences are part of my continued growth. I choose to release the guilt and shame I have for any perceived failures.

I accept all my actions in the world as perfect and right for the given moment.

I forgive and release myself from anxiety, self-limitations, guilt and other non-loving judgments regarding my value to myself and others.

As I release my loving intention today, I honor my true self and request balanced responsibility and wisdom in my life to hear, know and embrace that which is mine to do.

No more and no less.

Thank you, Thank you, Thank you and So Let It Be.

(Take a final deep breath and release it completing your intention)

Personal Affirmation Notes

(Use this space to record your thoughts, feelings and experiences.)

Greater Connection to Others

Instructions:
Create the proper intention in your mind (pg. 54). Do the breathing technique to generate spiritual energy (pg. 55). Say out loud before beginning: "I now gain access to my Akashic Field. I send the spiritual energy I have created to my Akashic Field for the purpose of the following affirmation."

Visualize the words as you express them out loud:

I am love. I am divine. I am connected to my greater knowing.

I see divine light pouring through me from the top of my head all the way to my feet granting me complete connection to others in my life.

I see my higher self guiding me through the journey of my life. I open my heart to receive all wisdom and connect consciously to my true self now. I see this connection open fully and completely as I go through my day.

I realize that I am not separate from the divine, my own self or any person that is presently in my life experience. My separation feelings have been an illusion created by my fears. I consciously and willingly let go of that so that I can expand my consciousness and establish a greater connection in my life.

I choose to have greater clarity and courage when dealing with life situations involving other people. I choose to see the greater purpose in all of my growth opportunities with them.

I am love. I am divine. I am connected to my greater knowing.

Thank you, Thank you, Thank you and So Let It Be.

(Take a final deep breath and release it completing your intention)

Personal Affirmation Notes

(Use this space to record your thoughts, feelings and experiences.)

Manifesting Abundance

Instructions:
Create the proper intention in your mind (pg. 54). Do the breathing technique to generate spiritual energy (pg. 55). Say out loud before beginning: "I now gain access to my Akashic Field. I send the spiritual energy I have created to my Akashic Field for the purpose of the following affirmation."

Visualize the words as you express them out loud:

I acknowledge the past parts of my life where I felt limited by feeling unsuccessful at manifesting my true purpose in life.

I visualize and see all of my previously blocked energies regarding my own manifestation of abundance.

I identify and release any vows of poverty that may be blocking me from prosperity in my life.

I release and change limiting patterns now from the dark patterns of fear into beautiful light patterns consisting of divine love, light and truth.

I accept healing at all areas of my life where I limit myself and my divine potential. I desire to be unlimited in the areas of personal and spiritual success.

I now allow myself to manifest whatever I truly need and accept those miracles that happen as my highest good.

I see my life free and full of abundance.

I am ready to receive all the gifts from the divine returning to me in my world through unconditional love and compassion.

Thank you, Thank you, Thank you and So Let It Be.

(Take a final deep breath and release it completing your intention)

Personal Affirmation Notes

(Use this space to record your thoughts, feelings and experiences.)

Healing & Overcoming Grief

Instructions:
Create the proper intention in your mind (pg. 54). Do the breathing technique to generate spiritual energy (pg. 55). Say out loud before beginning: "I now gain access to my Akashic Field. I send the spiritual energy I have created to my Akashic Field for the purpose of the following affirmation."

Visualize the words as you express them out loud:

I acknowledge my past grief, my pain and my loss. These losses have affected me and have been difficult to heal and resolve.

I know that I have the right to experience my grief as a process of letting go of my pain and healing my heart. In the past I have continued to carry this pain without a care for myself and the happiness I truly deserve.

I now desire with my heart to release and transmute the pain I have felt from a loss of a loved one, loss of livelihood, loss of freedom or other loss that has hurt me so deeply.

Please carry divine love to all areas of my being that are fractured by the pain I have felt. Please assist my heart to be whole and healed.

I honor the memory of my past while allowing myself to move forward from my past hurts. I choose freedom from my grief in order to grow and attain the happiness I deserve.

I am unconditional love and can receive this love in all areas of my life.

Thank you, Thank you, Thank you and So Let It Be.

(Take a final deep breath and release it completing your intention)

Personal Affirmation Notes

(Use this space to record your thoughts, feelings and experiences.)

Increasing Positive Perception

Instructions:
Create the proper intention in your mind (pg. 54). Do the breathing technique to generate spiritual energy (pg. 55). Say out loud before beginning: "I now gain access to my Akashic Field. I send the spiritual energy I have created to my Akashic Field for the purpose of the following affirmation."

Visualize the words as you express them out loud:

My past fears have allowed me to continue a view point of negativity in the major areas of my life. I desire to begin the shift from this negativity toward the positive expression of my true nature.

I desire to have all areas where I express negativity revealed to me so that I may actively change those thoughts to a positive. I choose to change fear to love, avoidance to courage, anger to peace and so forth.

Negativity blocks my manifestation of what I want to create in my life. Positive thoughts allow for me to open myself to greater possibilities in the future experiences of my life.

I acknowledge there are always different ways to view my life situations. I can choose to see the positive or choose to see the negative.

My desire over time is to begin to see the positive that can come from all life situations.

I choose to see the greater good in all areas of my life. I surrender to the divine plan for my life.

Thank you, Thank you, Thank you and So Let It Be.

(Take a final deep breath and release it completing your intention)

Personal Affirmation Notes

(Use this space to record your thoughts, feelings and experiences.)

Increasing Belief in Being Capable

Instructions:
Create the proper intention in your mind (pg. 54). Do the breathing technique to generate spiritual energy (pg. 55). Say out loud before beginning: "I now gain access to my Akashic Field. I send the spiritual energy I have created to my Akashic Field for the purpose of the following affirmation."

Visualize the words as you express them out loud:

I acknowledge the times when I feel overwhelmed or have increased anxiety and worry in my life. These feelings have affected my ability to feel secure and capable to deal with all life situations.

At times I feel unworthy to receive love and compassion. I feel alone and unable to receive assistance from the divine or others in my life. I try to take everything as a weight on my own shoulders.

I desire to open myself to the help that is available to me and clear those limiting beliefs that keep me separate from my true self and others.

I am worthy of a compassionate connection to all living beings.

I am capable to accomplish everything I have to do in the perfect time and place. I am successful in balancing my needs and the needs of others. I release my overwhelming burden and see it transmuted to divine love and light.

I move forward in my life allowing doubt, worry and anxiety to be recognized and changed to confidence, calm and peace. I see everything and every situation as perfect for me at this moment in time.

Thank you, Thank you, Thank you and So Let It Be.

(Take a final deep breath and release it completing your intention)

Personal Affirmation Notes

(Use this space to record your thoughts, feelings and experiences.)

Open Your Ability to Receive

Instructions:
Create the proper intention in your mind (pg. 54). Do the breathing technique to generate spiritual energy (pg. 55). Say out loud before beginning: "I now gain access to my Akashic Field. I send the spiritual energy I have created to my Akashic Field for the purpose of the following affirmation."

Visualize the words as you express them out loud:

I am love. I am divine. I am connected to my greater knowing.

I am ready to receive fully from those around me.

I see all people in my life coming to me with abundant gifts of friendship, love, caring and compassion.

They accept me for the wonderful gifts that I have deep inside me.

I realize I am worthy to receive abundantly in my life and release all fears I have associated with allowing others to care for me.

Each moment in my life is a gift that I freely embrace as I continue my journey of learning in my life.

I choose to open myself more each day with courage. I want to experience in my life that which I truly deserve. I see many gifts coming to me from all directions in my life bringing me exactly what I need each day.

I seek a perfect spiritual balance between the good I give to the world and the gifts I receive each day.

Thank you, Thank you, Thank you and So Let It Be.

(Take a final deep breath and release it completing your intention)

Personal Affirmation Notes

(Use this space to record your thoughts, feelings and experiences.)

Ending Belief in Suffering

Instructions:
Create the proper intention in your mind (pg. 54). Do the breathing technique to generate spiritual energy (pg. 55). Say out loud before beginning: "I now gain access to my Akashic Field. I send the spiritual energy I have created to my Akashic Field for the purpose of the following affirmation."

Visualize the words as you express them out loud:

I am love. I am divine. I am connected to my greater knowing.

I see divine light pouring through me from the top of my head all the way to my feet granting me complete connection to my authentic nature.

I see my higher self guiding me through the journey of my life. I open my heart to receive the gifts of worthiness and connect consciously to my true self now. I see this connection open fully and completely as I go through my day.

I realize that I do not need to create my own suffering to gain my worthiness and receive abundance in my life. My belief in suffering has been an illusion created by my fears.

I realize now that I do not need to suffer needlessly to attain what I desire to create in my life. I consciously and willingly let go of that so that I can expand my consciousness and establish a greater connection to manifestation in my life.

I choose to see my infinite worthiness in all aspects of my life: in myself, from others, with family, friends, career and my divine path.

I am love. I am divine. I am connected to my greater knowing.

Thank you, Thank you, Thank you and So Let It Be.

(Take a final deep breath and release it completing your intention)

Personal Affirmation Notes

(Use this space to record your thoughts, feelings and experiences.)

Healing Past Hurts

Instructions:
Create the proper intention in your mind (pg. 54). Do the breathing technique to generate spiritual energy (pg. 55). Say out loud before beginning: "I now gain access to my Akashic Field. I send the spiritual energy I have created to my Akashic Field for the purpose of the following affirmation."

Visualize the words as you express them out loud:

I am love. I am divine. I am connected to my greater knowing.

I am ready and willing to heal the past hurts in my lifetimes that presently block the expression of positive energy in my life.

I see all people in my life coming to me with abundant gifts of friendship, love, caring and compassion.

I ask for divine wisdom to see the perfect rhythm in my life and gain understanding about the purpose for all the situations in my life.

I realize I am worthy to receive abundantly in my life and release all fears I have associated with allowing myself to be free of my past.

I see all those who hurt me as my teachers, helping me to see life with greater clarity. I ask for the courage to heal my hurts. I ask for the wisdom to discern the best path to take in order to clear all situations and not allow them to be carried into the future.

I open myself to receive the healing energy of compassion that is pouring from life to me. I willingly allow it to help me balance the energies of my life.

I move forward in love and compassion for myself and others.

Thank you, Thank you, Thank you and So Let It Be.

(Take a final deep breath and release it completing your intention)

Personal Affirmation Notes

(Use this space to record your thoughts, feelings and experiences.)

Increasing Personal Responsibility

Instructions:
Create the proper intention in your mind (pg. 54). Do the breathing technique to generate spiritual energy (pg. 55). Say out loud before beginning: "I now gain access to my Akashic Field. I send the spiritual energy I have created to my Akashic Field for the purpose of the following affirmation."

Visualize the words as you express them out loud:

I accept responsibility in my life for all the choices I make regardless of the outcome.

I am perfect just as I am. My life will be filled with triumphs and what I perceive as negative outcomes.

I will learn from all life situations that present themselves.

I will make choices ultimately that are in my highest good.

I choose not to blame others for situations that I have created through my willing actions.

I choose to learn from every opportunity and embrace life fully.

I know that all life situations work toward the higher good whether I can fully see the purpose at this time.

I embrace growth, awareness and personal responsibility in my life.

Thank you, Thank you, Thank you and So Let It Be.

(Take a final deep breath and release it completing your intention)

Personal Affirmation Notes

(Use this space to record your thoughts, feelings and experiences.)

Chapter Eight

Affirmations for Creating Positive Growth

"Believe it is possible to solve your problem.
Tremendous things happen to the believer.
So believe the answer will come. It will"

~ Norman Vincent Peale

Consciously generating more positive spiritual energy within yo Field can translate to a more healthy future for you. When directly with the Akashic Field in a conscious manner, you can no clear unresolved past negative issues but program it with increased positive potentials for your world through your own intention.

Working directly with your intention to program more positive energies into the Akashic Field can transmute additional negative energies and allow you to create the future you deserve. It can also help you to become freer from subconscious blocks or barriers.

The key is consistent and clear positive thoughts with directed daily awareness and intention towards your Akashic Field. This can be very challenging in our very busy lifestyles. Even taking time each day to remain aware of the Akashic Field can help you free up and resolve energy in your life.

Setting aside some designated time for yourself either in meditation or using the affirmations in this book can start you toward the path of conscious creation in your life. It's like anything else, the more you put into it the more benefit you get out of it.

What we are able to see in our lives as potential realities is governed by the amount of both positive and negative energies in our Akashic Field. The more unresolved or negatively stored patterns, the harder it is for us to gain access to positive potentials for growth in our life.

The chart below contains 10 Akashic Field Affirmations for setting positive intentions and assisting with your spiritual growth.

Balancing Subtle Energies

Instructions:
Create the proper intention in your mind (pg. 54). Do the breathing technique to generate spiritual energy (pg. 55). Say out loud before beginning: "I now gain access to my Akashic Field. I send the spiritual energy I have created to my Akashic Field for the purpose of the following affirmation."

Visualize the words as you express them out loud:

I acknowledge all my energies as they radiate and eventually return to me in my life.

I acknowledge all subconscious beliefs and patterns that block the flow and expression of positive energy in my life.

I choose to release all negative energies that prohibit me from balancing all the subtle energies that are a part of me.

I visualize and see all of my subtle energy centers completely functional and open to receive energy fully from all of creation. I send my own energy to those chakra centers that are not moving as freely as they should be and have been blocked in the past by negative energies.

I visualize and see all of my endocrine glands completely free to radiate spiritual energy into the world around me. I send divine energies to those endocrine glands that may be blocked from expressing all energies that are possible.

I accept healing at all levels in these areas now and see them balanced and fully open.

I receive all the gifts from the world returning to me in love.
I radiate my light into the world sharing unconditional love with myself and others.

Thank you, Thank you, Thank you and So Let It Be.

(Take a final deep breath and release it completing your intention)

Personal Affirmation Notes

(Use this space to record your thoughts, feelings and experiences.)

Clearing Negative Energies

…oper intention in your mind (pg. 54). Do the breathing technique to … spiritual energy (pg. 55). Say out loud before beginning: "I now gain …s to my Akashic Field. I send the spiritual energy I have created to my …kashic Field for the purpose of the following affirmation."

Visualize the words as you express them out loud:

I acknowledge the areas of my life affected by negative energies and those currently creating discord in my subtle energies.

I see divine love and light fully surround me in the power of unconditional love. I deserve this universal gift in my daily life.

I desire to release all residual negative effects of trauma, judgment, discord, disruption and non-harmonious energies. I ask for healing to all areas affected by negative energy.

As I go through my day, I ask for white light to surround me and transmute all negative energies that may be created by myself or others.

I ask for wisdom to recognize negative energy in my daily life. I request the power to transform it immediately to positive growth opportunity.

I am unconditional love. I am surrounded by the light of creation. I am positive in all aspects of my life. My true path is illuminated always.

Thank you, Thank you, Thank you and So Let It Be.

(Take a final deep breath and release it completing your intention)

Personal Affirmation Notes

(Use this space to record your thoughts, feelings and experiences.)

Connecting to the Global Community

Instructions:
Create the proper intention in your mind (pg. 54). Do the breathing technique to generate spiritual energy (pg. 55). Say out loud before beginning: "I now gain access to my Akashic Field. I send the spiritual energy I have created to my Akashic Field for the purpose of the following affirmation."

Visualize the words as you express them out loud:

I am connected to all living beings that were born of the same universal breath of creation.

I know in my heart we are all one within our life circumstances.

Our oneness allows our hearts to spread unconditional love to those that need it. I connect to my global community so that I may be of service to the world.

I am grateful for my spiritual gifts. I desire to more willingly share them with the world around me so that I may take my place with others all over the world in divine service.

I send peace to all areas of the world that are struggling with war, famine, poverty, violence and other tragedy.

I see my love surround all these places and help to release negative energies. I see my love blend with others of the global community and make a profound difference.

I send my light now into this room, through my living space, to my neighborhood, to my city, to my state, to my country, eventually covering the entire planet.

I am part of the global community. I am one with all creation.

Thank you, Thank you, Thank you and So Let It Be.

(Take a final deep breath and release it completing your intention)

Personal Affirmation Notes

(Use this space to record your thoughts, feelings and experiences.)

Creating Healthy Relationships

Instructions:
Create the proper intention in your mind (pg. 54). Do the breathing technique to generate spiritual energy (pg. 55). Say out loud before beginning: "I now gain access to my Akashic Field. I send the spiritual energy I have created to my Akashic Field for the purpose of the following affirmation."

Visualize the words as you express them out loud:

I see divine light pouring through me from the top of my head all the way to my feet. This white light surrounds and enfolds me. It keeps me safe and is comfortable to me as I breathe in unconditional love.

I acknowledge my past issues and traumas surrounding relationships. I know holding on to these patterns and beliefs will block my ability to seek and find the right and perfect life partner for me. I consciously release all limiting patterns surrounding relationships.

I visualize and see all these negative relationship beliefs and patterns lifted away from me. I see this allow greater potentials for me in my life.

I request the release of any patterns that I am still unaware of at this time that may be blocking me from creating healthy relationships.

I acknowledge that I am connected to all my inherent divine wisdom. I release control over events, time frames and circumstances regarding the appearance of a perfect partner in my life and the creation of other healthy relationships.

I consciously remain open to allow the true unfolding of whatever is perfect and right for me.

I am love. I am divine. I am connected to my greater knowing.

Thank you, Thank you, Thank you and So Let It Be.

(Take a final deep breath and release it completing your intention)

Personal Affirmation Notes

(Use this space to record your thoughts, feelings and experiences.)

Expanding Spiritual Awareness

Instructions:
Create the proper intention in your mind (pg. 54). Do the breathing technique to generate spiritual energy (pg. 55). Say out loud before beginning: "I now gain access to my Akashic Field. I send the spiritual energy I have created to my Akashic Field for the purpose of the following affirmation."

Visualize the words as you express them out loud:

There are many illusions created by fear that block my own spiritual awareness.

I set my intention to have spiritual truth revealed to me in my life. I trust that others are the mirror for what I most need to see. I accept the lessons they bring to me regardless of how they happen in my life.

I desire for my spiritual awareness will be expanded so that I can participate in my necessary growth and learning.

I no longer wish to avoid, to hide or not to participate in those situations that are in my highest good.

I realize that there are many different ways to perceive life situations. I pledge to try and see all situations from an expanded point of view.

I ask universal energies to carry my intentions and support my expanding spiritual awareness in the days to come.

Thank you, Thank you, Thank you and So Let It Be.

(Take a final deep breath and release it completing your intention)

Personal Affirmation Notes

(Use this space to record your thoughts, feelings and experiences.)

Greater Connection to Higher Self

Instructions:
Create the proper intention in your mind (pg. 54). Do the breathing technique to generate spiritual energy (pg. 55). Say out loud before beginning: "I now gain access to my Akashic Field. I send the spiritual energy I have created to my Akashic Field for the purpose of the following affirmation."

Visualize the words as you express them out loud:

I am love. I am divine. I am connected to my greater knowing.

I see divine light pouring through me from the top of my head all the way to my feet. This white light surrounds and enfolds me. It keeps me safe and is comfortable to me as I breathe in unconditional love.

I see my higher self guiding me through the journey of my life. I open my heart to receive all wisdom and connect consciously to my true self now. I see this connection open fully and completely as I go through my day.

I visualize and see all of my subtle energy centers completely functional and open to receive energy fully from all of creation. I send my own energy to those chakra centers that are not moving as freely as they should be and have been blocked in the past by negative energies.

I visualize and see all of my endocrine energy centers completely functional and open to radiate my spiritual light into all of creation. I send my own energy to those endocrine centers that are not radiating as freely as they should be and have been blocked in the past by negative energies.

I consciously remain open to give this light to everyone in my life after giving it to myself.

I am love. I am divine. I am connected to my greater knowing.

Thank you, Thank you, Thank you and So Let It Be.

(Take a final deep breath and release it completing your intention)

Personal Affirmation Notes

(Use this space to record your thoughts, feelings and experiences.)

Opening to Greater Compassion

Instructions:
Create the proper intention in your mind (pg. 54). Do the breathing technique to generate spiritual energy (pg. 55). Say out loud before beginning: "I now gain access to my Akashic Field. I send the spiritual energy I have created to my Akashic Field for the purpose of the following affirmation."

Visualize the words as you express them out loud:

All the divine gifts of life flow from the ability to share compassion.

I see compassion flow into me and heal those areas of my life where I feel that I do not receive peace and love from others.

I set my intention toward showing myself greater compassion and understanding each day. I choose compassion for myself rather than judgment.

I desire wisdom to allow me to offer compassion to those that I love, those that I fear, those that I dislike and those I do not even know.

I ask universal energies to light my way toward greater compassion in my life. I know that compassion given freely will be returned to me 10 fold and that greater compassion will help to change the world in countless ways.

I send peace and compassion to all areas of the world in unrest and turmoil. I send peace and compassion to all areas of my own life that are filled with conflict.

I grant myself infinite compassion to do all that is in my highest good to do in this life now and for all my days.

Thank you, Thank you, Thank you and So Let It Be.

(Take a final deep breath and release it completing your intention)

Personal Affirmation Notes

(Use this space to record your thoughts, feelings and experiences.)

Illuminating Your True Path

Instructions:

Create the proper intention in your mind (pg. 54). Do the breathing technique to generate spiritual energy (pg. 55). Say out loud before beginning: "I now gain access to my Akashic Field. I send the spiritual energy I have created to my Akashic Field for the purpose of the following affirmation."

Visualize the words as you express them out loud:

Please remove all my limited perceptions in my life situations. Open my consciousness to allow for greater possibilities at all levels of thought and action.

I ask all divine energies available to me and open myself to receive this energy at all levels.

Allow my awareness to be completely opened now in order to reveal my true, authentic nature in all areas of my life.

Allow my path and purpose to be communicated with clarity of spirit, mind and body.

I consciously release all patterns of fear that may be associated with their true path and purpose.

Help to illuminate my true path under all conditions.

Thank you, Thank you, Thank you and So Let It Be.

(Take a final deep breath and release it completing your intention)

Personal Affirmation Notes

(Use this space to record your thoughts, feelings and experiences.)

Increasing Generosity

Instructions:
Create the proper intention in your mind (pg. 54). Do the breathing technique to generate spiritual energy (pg. 55). Say out loud before beginning: "I now gain access to my Akashic Field. I send the spiritual energy I have created to my Akashic Field for the purpose of the following affirmation."

Visualize the words as you express them out loud:

I desire to access the river of free flowing abundance in all areas of spirit, mind and body.

I ask for healing now in those areas of my life where I feel that I do not feel ready to receive gifts of love, peace and friendship from others.

I set my intention toward showing myself greater generosity so that I may offer this to others.

I desire greater wisdom to allow me to offer my generosity to those that I love, those that I fear, those that I dislike and those I do not even know.

I ask universal energies to light my way toward greater generosity in my life. I know that my ability to show greater generosity will be returned to me ten fold.

I trust that my ability to be generous in thought, word and deed will help guide others to more generosity in their lives.

I grant myself the gift of generosity to do all that is in my highest good to do in this life now and for all my days.

Thank you, Thank you, Thank you and So Let It Be.

(Take a final deep breath and release it completing your intention)

Personal Affirmation Notes

(Use this space to record your thoughts, feelings and experiences.)

Setting Positive Daily Intentions

Instructions:
Create the proper intention in your mind (pg. 54). Do the breathing technique to generate spiritual energy (pg. 55). Say out loud before beginning: "I now gain access to my Akashic Field. I send the spiritual energy I have created to my Akashic Field for the purpose of the following affirmation."

Visualize the words as you express them out loud:

As I begin each new day, I express my desire to set positive potentials into my Akashic Field.

I ask that these intentions be accessed and honored by my subconscious and that positive aspects of life enter my consciousness today.

Allow me to greet each experience with excitement and openness to greater learning.

I desire clarity in all life situations on this day and take responsibility for all my choices and subsequent actions.

I choose today to express my spiritual nature in all events that unfold today for my greater good.

I choose to see all people in my experiences as my greatest teachers.

I express divine love for myself and others.

I set my intention today for greater compassion to be expressed through me to all I encounter.

I am love. I am divine. I am connected to my greater knowing.

Thank you, Thank you, Thank you and So Let It Be.

(Take a final deep breath and release it completing your intention)

Personal Affirmation Notes

(Use this space to record your thoughts, feelings and experiences.)

Chapter Nine
Create a Happier Future

"Realization has no value until it's lived. That's how it is born into the world."

~ Byron Katie

I often think about all the people in my life. I wonder what portion o time they are truly happy. Repeated unhappiness can be caused by many unresolved issues and patterns of behavior in our lives. Our minds can become filled with so much information it can become unclear or fuzzy.

Each new day can be so challenging when we do not stop and consider what we are experiencing each moment. This is unfortunate since it's important to remember that all of us are beautiful children from a divine source. We are all very intuitive and powerful.

These gifts are not just reserved for those that we know to be "psychic" or "spiritual healers". All such spiritual resources such as intuition, divine wisdom and creativity are available to anyone regardless of upbringing, religious background or previous life choices.

The bottom line is: We all deserve happiness and peace in our lives. The biggest question I asked myself and my clients have asked me is: *How do I create a happier future free from my prior emotional burdens?*

As mentioned in a previous chapter, the way that I eventually became free of a lot of past trauma and emotional issues was by making an effort to be more conscious and fully present each day. We can only track our thoughts when we do this.

It is so important to be able to identify how we feel, what we are thinking and what our available choices are. Secondary to that is the ability to shift our initial perceptions of life to a much broader view. Clearing and resolving anything we have left undone or not expressed is very important to our future.

The Akashic Field is the source of all our experiences. Everything that may be affecting our present moment and future is ultimately found within our life hologram. Working with this energy can facilitate greater healing and well being in our lives.

Something I learned that became very important to me was that I had the power to make positive choices regardless of the life experience. It can seem at times we are limited in our options but this is an illusion created by unresolved trauma and other negative Akashic Field energies.

I am glad that I finally figured out that happiness versus unhappiness is a choice I can make in response to whatever is going on. Each of us has a nd a million different ways to live it. What choice we make antially affects all future events in our lifetime.

create a future of happiness? How do we start to shift the energy in our life so that the number of positive experiences outweighs the negative or traumatic?

The biggest action you can make about changing your life is simply start somewhere, anywhere. Nothing happens without a conscious action on your part. Nothing good can be gained without some type of effort. What stops us is the daunting way our past can loom over us and the hopeless feelings we can have when we can't figure out what to do or where to begin. This is why sometimes we never get anywhere and nothing really changes.

In my client practice, I only recommend those tools I've worked with personally. I've made a list of some ideas for you that helped me to overcome many of my own obstacles to happiness. These are important things to remember as you strive for greater consciousness in your life experiences.

Learn to Let Go

We all have attachments to many things. Let go of your expectations. Let go of your need to know everything. Set yourself free of worries or feelings that something may not go well. Be open to greater opportunities for growth and learning.

Let yourself make mistakes

We all expect children to make mistakes but do we allow for our own mistakes? We sometimes expect perfection for ourselves while allowing others the room to grow. Learn to look at shortcomings as an opportunity for growth and insight into future choices. If you practice this way to relax a bit with life, you will eventually see that there are no mistakes, only growth opportunities. In order to learn, we must have some experiences where we feel we'd like to make different choices if experienced again.

Laugh more

Our hectic lives, financial stresses, fast paced jobs and our increasing obligations do not allow for much rest and relaxation. We should make time for greater play and enjoyment. Read a book, allow time for your hobbies, make time for recreation and enjoy those around you. Sometimes laughter is truly the best medicine.

You never know how much time you have in you[...] should enjoy it.

Look at conflicting situations in a new way
There will always be conflicts and challenges in [...] triggered emotionally it's so easy to get stuck in a sin[...] view. We can make assumptions about the circumstances an[...] happened. After resolving your emotions and working through them, challenge yourself to step outside the situation and change what you think about it. Are you making assumptions about why the other person did what they did? Are you taking on too much? Did you really listen? What can you do to help yourself and the other person involved?

Recognize your thoughts
I cannot stress enough the importance of trying to track or be more conscious of your thoughts. So many thoughts run past us so quickly that we are not aware of what is going on in our mind during important moments in our life. It's also important not to judge our thoughts as "good" or "bad", simply to be aware. When you recognize a thought then ask yourself if that thought is positive or negative. If it's negative, then think about what thought you'd choose to replace it.

Do good things for yourself
We have all heard of "random acts of kindness". Performing acts of kindness can be applied to yourself as well. When I was going through a very low period in my life and didn't feel very confident, I practiced doing something weekly for myself that simply made me feel good. I bought myself a bouquet of flowers as a wonderful reminder that I was special and important. There are numerous ways to do good for ourselves. Try writing inspirational notes to yourself on self-stick notes and putting them in different areas where you'll see them during the day.

Be more understanding of yourself and others
Regardless of our actions, all of us are ultimately trying to grow, learn and become more of who we really are. It's important to practice compassion in difficult moments and learn to see others as a mirror for ourselves. Letting ourselves "off the hook" can also let us be more compassionate in our lives. We will all make choices we wish we had made differently. It's most important to understand the choices we make and know what choices we'd make different in the future.

lieve that there is meaning in everything and watch for it

.here is a subtle dance of energy flowing through life and everything that happens. I often call this the divine flow. Life communicates in different ways what we most need to know. Set your intention to see these subtle signs. Look for meaning in seemingly random events and you may be very surprised. I learned to pay attention to everything in my life and trusted that every moment had a meaning. Don't drive yourself crazy searching or you won't see what you need to. Simply try to relax and trust that there are more than obvious ways to be led to the correct path and right choices for you.

No progress is insignificant

We can be so hard on ourselves when we do things more than once even if we made a decision not to do them again. Often there are layers to our learning process and even if something that happens seems like a repeat of exactly the same thing, it's generally not. Simply being more aware is great progress going in the right direction. Give yourself compassionate room to grow at the pace that is best for you.

Setting Goals/Make a Clear Plan

Making clear, concise goals is a wonderful way to make a plan for your life and what you want to accomplish. Get to know what you'd like to create in your future. Try making three lists.

Make the first list of those areas or issues in your life that do not work well for you. Be sure to be specific. Second, make a list of whatever you feel are your assets and work well for you. Then looking at those two lists, make a list of your goals for improving the areas that don't work well. Some examples of plans for improving areas could be more open communication, reaching out to others when you need help, spending more time doing what you love, journaling, being kinder to yourself and so on.

Keep a Journal

Journaling is the way you can freely express yourself without fear of judgment. Try keeping a journal for 30 days. Write about your day. Write about the challenging situations that occurred. Write about whatever pops in your mind. After the 30 days, go back and read the pages. Ask yourself questions like: do I still feel the way I did then, what else could I have done in this situation differently, what did I discover about who I am, did I learn anything new about myself or others? You may be surprised about what true insights can come from journaling. If writing it out by hand is too hard for you, try typing it. That's how I journal. Try to journal for 15-30 minutes each session. Don't worry if you skip a day, but get back to when you can.

These suggestions may not be new ideas for you to consider. I realize that many of these suggestions can be found in various self help techniques.

Our minds can pass over these suggestions too quickly at times because we feel they are simply cliché. Cliché or not, they do have truth in them and really work for a majority of the people.

I am so convinced from my work with the Akashic Field that EVERYONE has the ability to grow, become intuitive and become clearer about their life path and purpose. All people have the internal strength to face their trauma and resolve it.

With all future quantum possibilities simply awaiting us to call them into action within the Akashic Field, our possibilities for becoming true creators in our lives are limitless.

We are the only thing that can get in the way of calling those divine possibilities into action. Our unresolved traumas can block our positive perceptions about life and limit our available resources.

We have the power to gain greater insight and heal those areas that are blocking us from manifesting a reality we truly desire and deserve. As we get to know ourselves and our core issues, we have the ability to be liberated from these barriers.

Creating a happier future starts with a single choice to face our fears and our past. Working directly with the Akashic Field in a conscious way can help to move old negative energies to make room for positive future possibilities.

There are many ways to access the power of the Akashic Field in our lives. Working with the affirmations in this book is only one recommended method.

Here are some additional suggestions for working directly with the energy of the Akashic Field:

Conscious Awareness

Simply becoming more aware of the existence of the Akashic Field can set energy into motion. When we are not consciously aware of what we are experiencing, this can block life energy.

Thinking more often about the existence of the Akashic Field in your daily life will imprint your intention and allow more unresolved energy to be freed through your life situations.

When things get difficult in life remember that those situations are naturally designed to trigger whatever you need most. You are being granted the ability to see a new aspect of yourself or look at something in the past in a new way or gain a more open perception.

Setting a Daily Intention to Clear Blocking Patterns

Awaking each day with the desire or intention to clear up unresolved patterns can also set this powerful energy into motion.

You could do a small ritual around this intention such as lighting a candle and saying something like this:

> *"I light this candle to ask for healing all my unresolved traumas and past life events. I ask that this intention be carried to my Akashic Field for the purposes of revealing to me the truth of whatever I must understand in order to clear and resolve them fully and completely."*

Meditation Practice

Meditation can be a very good way in general to remain open and centered in your life. If you already have a meditation practice in place, take some time to visualize the Akashic Field and your connection to it.

If you don't already have a daily practice, try doing 15 minutes of meditation per day. There are days that I simply sit quietly and breath deeply (trying the breathing technique on page 54). I visualize this energy as white light being directed to my Akashic Field. I move this energy toward my unresolved issues and try to strengthen my connection to my hologram. I try to relax and open my own energy for this connection as much as I can during the time allowed. You can do this in whatever way you choose. Be creative! There's no way to do this improperly.